LAST STOP, CARNEGIE HALL

William A. Vacchiano,
Trumpet, New York Philharmonic, 1935–1973

$\mathscr{L}$AST STOP, $\mathscr{C}$ARNEGIE HALL

✦

New York Philharmonic Trumpeter William Vacchiano

✦

Brian A. Shook

North Texas Lives of Musicians Series #6

University of North Texas Press
Denton, Texas

Permissions:
University of North Texas Press
1155 Union Circle #311336
Denton, TX 76203-5017

The paper used in this book meets the minimum requirements of the American National Standard for Permanence of Paper for Printed Library Materials, z39.48.1984. Binding materials have been chosen for durability.

Library of Congress Cataloging-in-Publication Data

Shook, Brian A. (Brian Andrew), 1978-
Last stop, Carnegie Hall : New York Philharmonic trumpeter William Vacchiano / by Brian A. Shook. -- 1st ed.
  p. cm. -- (North Texas lives of musicians series ; #6)
«Foreword: Wynton Marsalis.»--T.p. verso.
Includes bibliographical references and index.
ISBN 978-1-57441-306-9 (cloth : alk. paper)
  1. Vacchiano, William. 2. Trumpet players--New York (State)--New York--Biography. 3. Trumpet--Instruction and study--United States. 4. New York Philharmonic--History--20th century. I. Title. II. Series: North Texas lives of musicians series ; no. 6.
ML419.V13S56 2011
788.9»2092--dc22
[B]
                                              2010044068

Last Stop, Carnegie Hall: New York Philharmonic Trumpeter William Vacchiano
is Number 6 in the North Texas Lives of Musicians Series

Arturo Toscanini's handwritten manuscript of the second cornet part from Verdi's *Don Carlos* in Chapter 3 is courtesy of Eileen Prager Perry. Used by permission.

All mouthpiece illustrations in Chapter 6 appear courtesy of Stork Custom Mouthpieces (http://www.storkcustom.com). Used by permission.

Bill—You said this to many others and I say it to you—
"Thanks a million."

$\mathcal{C}$ONTENTS

List of Illustrations x

Foreword by Wynton Marsalis xiii

Preface xv

Acknowledgments xvii

Introduction 1

Chapter 1: Biography 3

    Family History 3

    Early Studies and Performances in Portland and Boston 4

    The Road to New York 10

    Max Schlossberg and The Juilliard School 12

    A Dual Career as a Performer and Teacher 17

    Retirement Years (1973–2005) 24

Chapter 2: Vacchiano and the New York Philharmonic 28

    The New York Philharmonic 28

    Vacchiano's Perception of Various Conductors 29

    The Philharmonic Trumpet Section 34

    Vacchiano and Nat Prager 35

    Personal Impressions of Vacchiano's Musicianship 40

Chapter 3: Responsibilities of a Principal Trumpeter 49

    Principles of Orchestral Musicianship 49

    Vacchiano on Orchestral Excerpts 51

    Historical Background of Compositions 52

    Approach to Specific Styles and Excerpts 54

    Preparing for the Audition 56

Chapter 4: Vacchiano's Rules of Orchestral Performance 59

    Articulation 59

    Rhythm 62

Phrasing...64
Miscellaneous 65
Chapter 5: Pedagogical Methods 67
    Teaching Style 67
    Transposition...74
    Tone Production..76
    Intonation...77
    Tonguing 78
Chapter 6: Vacchiano's Use of Equipment.............81
    The Mouthpiece 81
    Rim Diameter...84
    Rim Shape and Contour....................................84
    The Cup..87
    Throat and Bore..90
    Backbore (Venturi) 91
    Trumpets in Various Keys..................................92
    Choosing the Right Equipment in an Orchestra 95
Chapter 7: Remembering Bill 100
    Philip Varriale's Eulogy 100
    Lee Soper's Memorial..105
    Presentation of Honorary Doctorate to
        William Vacchiano 107
    Personal Recollections from Former Students,
        Colleagues, and Friends 108

Appendix A:
    Principal and Guest Conductors of the
        New York Philharmonic, 1935–1973.........124
Appendix B:
    New York Philharmonic Trumpet Section,
        The Vacchiano Years, 1935–1973................127

Appendix C:
New York Philharmonic World Premières, 1935–1973 129
Appendix D:
New York Philharmonic U.S. Premières, 1935–1973........136
Appendix E:
Selected Discography of William Vacchiano with
the New York Philharmonic, 1935–1973....................141
Appendix F:
Bibliography of Music Publications by
William Vacchiano 157
Appendix G:
The Students of William Vacchiano 159

Endnotes 166
Bibliography and Sources 177
Index 185

Illustrations

1.1. Max Schlossberg, "Four-in-One" 15

1.2. Richard Strauss, *Der Rosenkavalier*, Trumpet in C 18

1.3. Claude Debussy, *La Mer*, Cornet in C 19

2.1. Richard Strauss, *Ein Heldenleben*, Trumpet in E 32

3.1. Ludwig van Beethoven, *Overture to "Leonore" No. 2*,
Trumpet in E-flat 55

3.2. Gustav Mahler, *Symphony No. 5*, Trumpet in B-flat 56

3.3. Giuseppe Verdi, *Don Carlos*, Act IV, Part 2,
Second Cornet in A 58

4.1. Slur Two, Tongue Two 59

4.2. Igor Stravinsky, *Petrouchka*, "Ballerina's Dance,"
Trumpet in B-flat 60

4.3. Long Slur, Short Slur... 60

4.4. Long Quarters, Short Eighths, Long Sixteenths 61

4.5. Richard Strauss, *Ein Heldenleben*, Trumpet in E 62

4.6. Modest Mussorgsky, *Pictures at an Exhibition*,
"Goldenberg and Schmuyle"... 64

4.7. Modest Mussorgsky, *Pictures at an Exhibition*,
"Promenade," Trumpet in C 65

4.8. Richard Strauss, *Symphonia Domestica*,
Exercise Variation 66

4.9. "A-men" Cadence 66

5.1. Jean-Baptiste Arban, *Method for Trumpet*, p. 40, #8 68

5.2. Jean-Baptiste Arban, *Method for Trumpet*, p. 73, #64,
Scales 68

5.3. Jean-Baptiste Arban, *Method for Trumpet*, p. 44, #22,
Slurs.. 69

5.4. Jean-Baptiste Arban, *Method for Trumpet*, p. 155, #1,
Triple Tongue 69

5.5. Jean-Baptiste Arban, *Method for Trumpet*, p. 142, #48,
Arpeggios 69

5.6. Jean-Baptiste Arban, *Method for Trumpet*, p. 125, #1,
Intervals 69

5.7. Dmitry Shostakovich, *Concerto for Piano, Trumpet, and
Strings*, Mvt. 3 79

5.8. Nikolay Rimsky-Korsakov, *Capriccio Espagnol*, Mvt. 3 80

6.1. Diagram of the Mouthpiece 83

6.2. High Point of the Rim 85

6.3. Cushion Rim 87

6.4. "C" Cup 88

6.5. "V-Shaped" Cup 88

6.6. Robert Schumann, *Symphony No. 2*, Trumpet in C 95

6.7. Pyotr Il'yich Tchaikovsky, *Capriccio Italien*, Cornet in A 96

6.8. Carl Maria von Weber, *Overture to "Oberon,"*
Trumpet in D 98

Photos

1. (frontisphoto) Vacchiano press photo

Photos after page 80:

2. Vacchiano in high school

3. Rafaello Vacchiano

4. Max Schlossberg

5. Ethel Josephine LaParde

6. Sketch of William Vacchiano

7. Vacchiano ca. 1940

8. Vacchiano headshot

9. Vacchiano in tobacco field

10. Vacchiano sitting on desk

11. Mayor LaGuardia with Philharmonic musicians

12. Vacchiano and the NYP Red Cross drive

13. Philharmonic principal musicians with Bruno Walter
14. Philharmonic trumpet section in rehearsal
15. Vacchiano in rehearsal
16. Vacchiano signing checks
17. New York Philharmonic brass, ca. 1958
18. Vacchiano with F trumpet
19. Vacchiano with multiple trumpets
20. Vacchiano in a Tokyo hotel, 1961
21. Johnny Ware, Ed Herman, and Vacchiano, ca. 1970
22. Maynard Ferguson, Vacchiano, and Charles Colin
23. Wynton Marsalis and Vacchiano
24. Vacchiano presenting a master class
25. Vacchiano with the Canadian Brass
26. Vacchiano, Thomas Stevens, Irving Bush, and Don Green
27. Frank Kaderabek, Vacchiano, and Armando Ghitalla
28. Vacchiano's 80ᵗʰ birthday
29. Chris Gekker, Mark Gould, Vacchiano, Ray Mase, Phil Smith
30. Vacchiano and Jonny Ware
31. John "Peppy" Pettinato
32. Vacchiano inspecting a trumpet
33. Vacchiano in 2001
34. Vacchiano receiving his Honorary Doctorate from The Juilliard School
35. Vacchiano at piano
36. Vacchiano in his teaching studio

$\mathcal{F}$OREWORD

During my teen years in New Orleans, my trumpet teacher was George Jansen. He had studied with William Vacchiano some twenty-five years earlier and recommended that I do the same in college. The first time I met Mr. Vacchiano was when I auditioned at Juilliard in 1979 (Gerard Schwarz and Edward Treutel were also there). I played Mussorgsky's *Pictures at an Exhibition*, Hummel's *Trumpet Concerto*, and Bach's *Brandenburg Concerto No. 2*. After the audition, as I walked out of the room, Vacchiano told me, "Tell George Jansen he was right." I had no idea what that meant. I later asked Mr. Jansen about Vacchiano's cryptic comment. He said he'd told Vacchiano I was a genius. I had already enjoyed a lot of success as a high school trumpeter, but I had no idea Mr. Jansen thought that highly of me, so that was quite a compliment coming from both of them.

I studied with Mr. Vacchiano at Juilliard from 1979 through 1980, and took a few lessons in 1981. He had retired from the New York Philharmonic before I got to Juilliard. We went through the standard books and excerpts and studied double and triple tonguing, transposition, how to approach certain types of music, and all kinds of technical things. He liked to write the number of each exercise on the inside flap of the book you were to work from. I still have the Saint-Jacome and Sachse books from those lessons. It's funny, but I hadn't thought about that until the moment I started considering my contribution to this book—over twenty years ago.

My lessons took on a new character once we got to know each other better. We had some differences of opinion, mainly about race and culture and America, I think he both enjoyed and didn't enjoy discussing them. We were from completely different generations and concepts. We never did agree on those issues, but I certainly respected him and think he respected me.

I had never visited his home in Flushing, New York, so a few years after I left Juilliard, I called him one day to see if I could go over for a lesson. He happily agreed and gave me directions to his house. I got there about 6:30 in the evening, and he invited me to sit down at the kitchen table. It had a lamp hanging over it; I can still remember it after all these years. We just sat at that table talking, but speaking in an intimate way, the way an older man talks to a younger one he loves. It was strange because we had never shared that type of feeling. He talked about the things that happened to him over the years—his life, his wife and her illness, and his son's death. I can still see it—just him and me, alone under that light, the rest of the house dark. "Marsalis, (he always called me by my last name) my wife is in that room. She has been an invalid for years and when she dies, I will be alone." He said, "You will be successful playing. You already are. But you live your life with the people around you. If your life with them is unhappy, you are unhappy. Take care of the people in your immediate environment and take care of yourself." Well, that advice affected me deeply.

I didn't leave until almost midnight and I never took out a trumpet.

I had a lot of lessons with Bill Vacchiano, but that evening he taught me the things I have reflected on most as the years have passed. If your internal life is happy, you are happy. Pay attention to the loved ones around you.

I went over there for a one-hour lesson, but instead he gave me more than an hour could possibly hold. Thinking about that night, about me and him in his lonely house, still brings tears to my eyes.

Wynton Marsalis
August 2010

$\mathscr{P}$REFACE

Few trumpet teachers influenced as many individual students professionally and personally as William Vacchiano, principal trumpet of
the New York Philharmonic (1935–1973). His contributions to the music world include hundreds of orchestral recordings, numerous method books, thousands of private students, and a lifetime of research on
trumpet mouthpieces resulting in his own line of mouthpieces (made
by Stork Custom Mouthpieces). He was a pillar of strength in one of
the world's most prominent orchestras during its burgeoning years of
prosperity, while simultaneously being the most sought-after trumpet
pedagogue in New York City. His teaching career lasted more than sev-
en decades, during which time he taught out of his home in Flushing,
New York, and served on the faculties at The Juilliard School, Manhattan School of Music, Mannes College of Music, Queens College, North
Carolina School of the Arts, and Columbia Teachers College. Among
his students are such famous musicians as Philip Smith, Miles Davis,
Thomas Stevens, Manny Laureano, Malcolm McNab, Gerard Schwarz,
and Wynton Marsalis.

While engaged at the Philharmonic, Vacchiano performed under
the baton of many legendary conductors like Arturo Toscanini, Bruno
Walter, Dimitri Mitropoulos, Leopold Stokowski, Leonard Bernstein,
and George Szell. The advent of broadcasts and recorded music created
new outlets for these conductors to demonstrate their interpretation, as
well as feature their orchestras with expansive literature. The exposure to
these musical giants enhanced Vacchiano's wisdom and understanding
of music that he imparted to his students. His teaching style was simple

and direct, focusing on musicianship and the fundamentals of trumpet playing. Upon finishing studies with Vacchiano, each student possessed the tools necessary to function and excel in the demanding profession of music.

Many of the methods Vacchiano used in his teaching and performing came from his teachers, but he also employed some new techniques that previously had only been experimental. In Vacchiano's orchestral performance he was one of the first principal trumpet players to use a variety of specialty trumpets in various keys, with the D trumpet eventually becoming his instrument of choice—especially for Mahler's symphonies.

Vacchiano was also the first trumpet teacher to go to considerable lengths in finding the right mouthpiece for each student. His knowledge, understanding, and expertise in this arena were unparalleled. Mouthpiece selection was a fundamental aspect of Vacchiano's teaching because he believed that if a student did not have the right mouthpiece he would never succeed, regardless of his dedication or talent.

The passion Vacchiano possessed for music was clearly evident in his performing and teaching. Listening to his recordings and talking to his students quickly reveals his dedication to music and personal connection with each student. The list of Vacchiano's students reads like a "Who's Who" among trumpet players. Exploring the reasons these individuals succeeded is paramount to understanding what is necessary for today's students to be successful as teachers and performers.

ACKNOWLEDGMENTS

Researching and communicating the life and career of Bill Vacchiano has touched me both musically and personally. I did not realize the number of individuals and organizations with which I would become so familiar over the years in preparing this book. A task this monumental would not be possible without the specific assistance of others.

A resource that I could not exhaust was the New York Philharmonic Archives where Richard Wandel and the rest of the staff patiently answered an endless number of questions and provided valuable information to ensure accuracy and authenticity of Bill's story. I would also like to thank Jeni Dahmus and Ray Mase from The Juilliard School for their help in providing detailed information regarding Bill's collegiate and teaching careers at Juilliard.

Many thanks goes to Allan Colin of Charles Colin Music Publications for his generosity in providing me with the entire Vacchiano music catalogue published by Charles Colin, as well as selected issues of the New York Brass Conference for Scholarships *Journal*. A special thanks to Phyllis Stork from Stork Custom Mouthpieces who kindly offered illustrations for the mouthpiece portion of this book—Bill's favorite topic.

On a personal level, I have had the privilege of working closely with a number of people I would have otherwise never met. To Lee Soper, whose tenderness and reverence for Bill was contagious and inspirational on a regular basis. To my mentor, colleague, and friend, David Hickman, for his guidance and constant support that continues to accompany me.

Two individuals who have been supremely important are Jo Ann Vacchiano and Anne Hardin. The kindness and affability of Jo Ann mirrors that of her father, and facilitated the continuation of my research after his passing. The hours we spent discussing her father's life and perusing pictures will forever be a fond memory.

Anne Hardin, former editor of the International Trumpet Guild *Journal*, has been a tremendous help in steering me through the in-depth process of publishing Bill's biography. From our first conversation I could tell we would not only be wonderful colleagues, but also life-long friends. Her detailed expertise, keen perceptions, and Southern charm cultivated assurance when I needed it most.

This book would not have been possible without the supervision of Karen DeVinney and the University of North Texas Press. Thank you for making Bill's dream and mine a reality.

To my parents and family for their unparalleled love and care for me and my endeavors. The interest and curiosity with which they followed this project has encouraged me more than they realize.

To my loving and patient wife Kristin for her endless confidence in me.

I wish to thank the multitude of Vacchiano students and colleagues who assisted me in my research. It has been a wonderful pleasure to get to know each of you and to view Bill through your eyes. I am amazed at the number of times I heard the phrase, "Bill was like a father to me"—and I now know why. May you always cherish his genuine musical parenting and pass it on to future generations.

As a tribute to Bill's teaching legacy and his dedication to his students, The Juilliard School established the William Vacchiano Award in Trumpet in 1991. This award grants scholarships to talented young trumpet players studying at Juilliard. Contributions can be sent to Ms. Tori Brand, Manager of Scholarship Development, The Juilliard School, 60 Lincoln Center Plaza, New York, NY USA 10023, or call (212) 799-5000, ext. 692.

Finally, I'd like to thank Bill Vacchiano, who so willingly gave his knowledge and ability to thousands of trumpet players, and who trusted me to tell his story. Bill humbly showed us all the meaning of being a consummate musician, full of personal and professional integrity. It was not only his musicianship that made him successful and influential, but also his strength of character and dedication to each individual. Bill was a *true* teacher whose impact will continue to be felt through his students for generations to come.

Brian A. Shook
January 2011

$\mathcal{I}$NTRODUCTION

I met William Vacchiano when he was ninety-one years old; I was twenty-four. I was a doctoral student in trumpet performance at Arizona State University, and my major professor, David Hickman, and I decided that writing a biography of a famous musician would be just the right fit for me and my interests. I compiled a list of prominent trumpet players who did not have an extended biography published on them and we began discussing the possibility of each for my project. When we got to William Vacchiano, Professor Hickman asked if any major research existed on him. I double-checked all my resources and could locate only a handful of articles—no official biography could be found. Mr. Hickman called William Vacchiano and proposed that I write his biography. Mr. Vacchiano warmly accepted this request.

I was quite nervous when I called Mr. Vacchiano for the first time because he had been retired from the New York Philharmonic for longer than I had been alive. My hands were cold and clammy and my heart was racing as I dialed his phone number. I briefly introduced myself and explained the purpose of the call. He was very friendly; the conversation couldn't have lasted more than five minutes. He agreed to some preliminary telephone interviews, and I set up several trips from Arizona to New York.

When I arrived in New York for the first interview, I phoned Mr. Vacchiano for directions to his house from the subway. He proceeded to give me *exact* directions as to which train to take, which end to get on, and how to exit the subway so that I surfaced in front of the appropriate bus stop. I got the distinct impression that describing the same route he spent so many years taking was a joy for him. His directions were perfect, and I got there like I'd been doing it all *my* life. When I rang the doorbell, Mr. Vacchiano came to the door, dressed in a tie and sweater, and he welcomed me into his home. His eyes were most striking—inviting, personal, gentle, and full of life. He showed me into his living room as he said, "Call me Bill." Getting started was as simple as that, and for the next two years he told me his stories, I interviewed friends and former students, and I did my research. Every time I worked on the project, a New York Philharmonic record was playing in the background. It was almost like having Bill in the room.

Initially, I set out to find as many of his professional accomplishments as possible in order to accent his career and exhibit his influence in the musical world. I did not get any further than the first interview with one of his students before realizing the depth of his humanity. Interview after interview was chock full of personal anecdotes of how Bill cared about each student as a person, not just as a musician.

Even though I never had the privilege of studying with Bill, he always treated me as if I was a part of his musical family. We exchanged letters and Christmas cards every year until he died in 2005. During one of my several visits to his home, Bill gave me a stack of all his personal notes from the various lectures he had given over the course of his illustrious career. Included with those notes was an unfinished autobiography he had called "Carnegie Hall: The Last Stop." This information became critical in my research and I wanted to honor him by incorporating his words with mine for the title of this book.

CHAPTER ONE

$\mathscr{B}$IOGRAPHY

✦

Family History

William Anthony Vacchiano was born on May 23, 1912, in Portland, Maine, the seventh of eight children to Rafaello and Anna Vacchiano. Of his seven siblings, Vacchiano had five older sisters, one older
brother, and one younger brother. The two oldest sisters, Mary and Margarita, were born in Italy before their parents immigrated to the United
States from their hometown of Cicciano, Italy. Vacchiano's father, Rafaello, was trained as a metal worker after serving as a member of the
King's Guard.[1] Eventually, Rafaello sailed for America where he hoped
to find more financial stability and a better life for his family. Many immigrants had various family members already living in America, which
made the move and transition easier. It was no different for Rafaello.
When he arrived at Ellis Island, he was greeted by his two brothers,
Megucia and Pasquale.[2]

Rafaello Vacchiano found a place to live on Atlantic Avenue in
Brooklyn and began working there as a grocer. A year later, after enough
money had been saved, he was able to pay for his wife and two daughters
to move to America. This trip was more difficult than the usual trans-
Atlantic crossing, for the ship, the *Ravelli*, developed rudder problems
and was forced to dock in order to make the appropriate repairs. It took
almost a month for parts to arrive and repairs to be made. Passengers

carried most of their own food and provisions, and few were prepared for this extra month of travel. When Vacchiano's mother and two sisters finally arrived they vowed never to set foot on a ship again. During the next several years, the Vacchiano family lived in Brooklyn where Vacchiano's three older sisters were born: Anna, Frances, and Nancy.[3]

Around 1909, the Vacchianos moved to Portland, Maine, where many friends from Italy were living. Vacchiano and his two brothers, Milo and Dominic, were born in Portland. Vacchiano vividly remembered this community where he grew up: "The sector of the city where we lived was like a part of Italy carved out and planted in Portland. All the customs, language, churches, and stores were strictly Italian. My father was an ardent fisherman and was very happy with the move. My mother was also content because most of her neighbors were from Italy."[4]

Early Studies and Performances
in Portland and Boston

Vacchiano's father recognized William's love of music when he was just a little boy. As early as age six, Rafaello took him to the Portland City Hall Auditorium to hear music. The first live performance he heard was Verdi's *La Traviata*, and he was thrilled with the sights and sounds that surrounded him.[5] The pervasiveness of the Italian culture in Portland exposed Vacchiano to a rich musical environment, serving as a catalyst to his career as a musician.

Vacchiano claimed that his career started by accident:

> My family lived in a house that was at the bottom of a very steep hill in Portland. I used to ride home from school on a bicycle without brakes, which meant I had to meander from side to side; otherwise I would have landed in the ocean that was close to my house! One day, a schoolmate and neighbor of mine, Louis Bennett, was carrying a baritone horn and got caught in my path. After I crashed into him, we realized I had

put a small dent in his horn and we both were terrified. I didn't know at the time that the dent could be removed with a drumstick, since brass is very soft. We both panicked and went to the teacher, Mr. DiNobile, to explain the dent. At the time, we were about eight or nine years of age, so we didn't understand how much it would cost to fix the horn. We thought we were in serious trouble. Mr. DiNobile was recruiting local youngsters for his band and he asked me if I would like to play an instrument. I grabbed the opportunity to get out of the scrape and said, "Yes!"[6]

Vacchiano continued:

Mr. DiNobile's teaching was very Italian. This method meant one year of solfège before starting on an instrument. I had five fifteen-minute lessons every day after school. After one year of rigorous study, he told me to ask my father what instrument I was to play. My five older sisters decided I was to play the saxophone which Rudy Vallee had made popular back then. My father agreed, but knew enough about music to know I had to start on clarinet. He pinned fifty dollars to the inside of my shirt and sent me off to my teacher who lived across the street from us. On the way to the teacher something distracted me—a ball game or something similar—and I arrived at his house one hour later. When he asked me what instrument my father selected, I couldn't remember. After calming me down he started to name instruments to see if I could remember what my father had said. He could have crossed the street and asked my father but my destiny was wrapped up in this little drama. My father spoke only Italian to me and to a nine-year old boy who knew nothing about instruments, the instrument my father named didn't make a deep impression on me.

The teacher started to name different instruments and he happened to start with the brass family. When he came to the *cornetto* I said, "That's it!" The difference between *cornetto* and *clarinetto* to a nine-year-old boy was indistinguishable. When I showed up at home with a cornet, my father was beside himself. "The instrument you want is black and made of wood!" My mother, who was preparing supper, interrupted by saying, "What's the difference? Cornet or clarinet, he's not going to be a professional." My father threw his hands and let the incident end there. As it turned out, I had a flair for the cornet and since I could read music well, soon I was playing first chair in the band.[7]

Mr. DiNobile stayed in America for only a couple more years before returning to Italy. Vacchiano needed to find a new teacher and soon started studying with Frank Knapp, who was his first cornet teacher. Vacchiano was about twelve years old when he began studying with him; Knapp was retired and in his seventies. During Knapp's career as a cornetist, he was solo cornet in Alessandro Liberati's band in New York. Liberati was one of the world's greatest cornet players. Interestingly, Liberati was principal trumpet (on cornet) with the Philharmonic Society of New York (which later became the New York Philharmonic) during the winter seasons of 1879 and 1880, the desk that Vacchiano was appointed to six decades later. Knapp made an indelible impression on Vacchiano at an early age. He said, "Mr. Knapp had the most beautiful sound I have ever heard."[8]

The most significant aspect of Knapp's influence and guidance on Vacchiano's early training occurred when Knapp appointed Vacchiano to third trumpet in the Portland Municipal Orchestra (now the Portland Symphony Orchestra). Knapp was principal trumpet and introduced Vacchiano to the trumpet section when he was only fourteen years old. This experience not only broadened Vacchiano's musical abilities, but also gave him the thrill of playing in a professional orchestra.

In addition to his studies with Knapp, Vacchiano also took piano lessons. As became evident later, the intense study of solfège and piano at an early age significantly enhanced Vacchiano's playing and teaching careers, especially with regard to transposition. The fee for his cornet lessons was two dollars, which was "a goodly sum in those days."[9] Due to the expenses involved in taking both piano and trumpet lessons, Vacchiano was forced to choose between them. "I sometimes feel sorry I didn't select the piano because I think the piano is a complete instrument. One can play a symphony on the piano. However, I believe in destiny as the rest of my saga will reveal."[10]

Vacchiano dedicated himself to music and Knapp quickly recognized the potential he possessed. To encourage his musical advancement, Knapp introduced him to the 240th Artillery Coast Guard Band in Portland. At the time, Vacchiano was only fourteen years old and was too young to play in any of the bands, but he looked older because he had a moustache. "When I told the security officer I was eighteen, he let me play with the band although he knew I was fibbing."[11]

In the summers, Vacchiano spent about four weeks at Camp Devons in Massachusetts where he played with the 240th Artillery Coast Guard Band, as well as with the Lewiston Artillery Band. These bands came to Camp Devons for National Guard training and rehearsed every week, earning Vacchiano five dollars for each rehearsal. "With all of these rehearsals, I made about ten or fifteen dollars a week, which was the average salary among the immigrants in those days."[12]

Vacchiano continued to acquire further experience at Portland High School by playing solos every Friday:

> In grade school, the custom was to assemble in the big auditorium every Friday morning to hear the legendary Walter Damrosch. It was a typical children's concert. Before the broadcast, the school band would march the students into the auditorium. I used to play a solo almost every Friday. By the end of high school I knew approximately sixty solos.[13]

Vacchiano maintained a rigorous practice schedule all through his high school years: from 2:00 P.M. to 3:00 P.M. was trumpet practice, 3:00 P.M. to 4:00 P.M. was homework, 4:00 P.M. to 5:00 P.M. was trumpet and 5:00 P.M. to 6:00 P.M. was piano, followed by more homework. "It was the custom for teachers to ask students to stay after school for extra help. One day, one of my teachers told me to stay for extra help. I said I couldn't because I had to practice. After that one time, I was never asked to stay for extra help again because I wanted to be able to practice all afternoon." [14]

During Vacchiano's last two years in high school, he commuted to Boston for lessons with Georges Mager, the great principal trumpet player of the Boston Symphony Orchestra (1919–1950).

> Georges Mager influenced my life more than anyone else. The equipment he was using [i.e. the mouthpiece] was what I should have been using, but I didn't realize it at the time. [His mouthpiece] doubled my sound, range, speed of tonguing. Everything opened right up! If I hadn't met him I probably never would have known these things were possible until, perhaps, much later in my life. [15]

It was around this same time that Vacchiano also took intermittent lessons with Louis Kloepfel and Walter M. Smith in Boston. Kloepfel had been principal trumpet with the New York Symphony Society (1891–1898), as well as with the Boston Symphony (1898–1914) and was retired when Vacchiano studied with him. Smith, former cornetist with the Sousa Band and also Solo Cornet with the U.S. Marine Band, had a significant impact on Vacchiano's career, not only with his teaching, but also with his method book, *Top Tones for the Trumpeter*, that Vacchiano used frequently in his own teaching.

Vacchiano devised a special routine in order to get to Boston for these lessons:

> When I was fourteen and still in high school, we lived only one hundred miles from Boston. In those depression days, they used to run excursions to get people to spend some money. To go from Portland to Boston cost only $2.00 round trip. I used to go down there every Saturday to take a lesson from the great Walter M. Smith, who was the outstanding soloist of the United States [Marine Band]. Meanwhile, I used to sneak over to see Louis Kloepfel. They were both fantastic teachers . . . equally as

famous as Schlossberg in New York. But that didn't go on for long as we couldn't afford the $2.00 carfare too often in those days.[16]

Vacchiano periodically studied with Gustav Heim, who had served as principal trumpet of almost every major orchestra in the country (Saint Louis Symphony Orchestra, 1904–1905; Philadelphia Orchestra, 1905–1906; Boston Symphony Orchestra, 1906–1920; Detroit Symphony Orchestra, 1920–1921; Philharmonic Society of New York, 1921–1923; Cleveland Orchestra, 1923–1924; and New York Symphony Society, 1925–1928). Mager was the teacher who helped Vacchiano find the right mouthpiece, but it was Heim who introduced the benefits of using higher pitched trumpets to Vacchiano. The magnificent combination of the instruction from these two famous players, Mager and Heim, had a tremendous impact on Vacchiano's career as a trumpet player and pedagogue for nearly seven decades.

> I owed practically all my success to [Gustav Heim]. I have attributed my long career to the ability to play all these [different pitched trumpets] and he taught me the proper way of doing it. I have a funny story about Gustav Heim. You weren't allowed to drink [alcohol] in those days, and he was a German up in the dry state of Maine. He used to make home-brew and they told him, "Gus, please don't make any home-brew and give it to the farmers. If you want to drink it, do it yourself." Well, he insisted and they put him in jail for four weeks. I went up there one day [for a lesson] and I couldn't find him. They told me he was over at the jail. So I went over [to the jail] and took a lesson [from him]. It was quite a memorable experience.[17]

Vacchiano's extensive experience and dedication at such a young age enabled him to thrive in New York's musical environment. "I didn't realize it until later but, by the time I came to New York, I was really a seasoned musician. In a small town like that, you just don't know. In a big city you can tell where you stand from your neighbors and friends. You can tell how well you play compared to them. But we had nothing to go by."[18]

While Vacchiano enjoyed his success as a legitimate trumpet player, he still faced the lure of being in a dance band and the attraction of receiving a higher wage. In an interview with Bill Spilka, Vacchiano related the following story:

> Isham Jones [1894–1956] was playing in Boston and asked Walter Smith if he knew a good, young trumpet player who might join his band for an engagement on the pier in Old Orchard, Maine, where all the big bands went to play. Walter gave him my name. When Jones passed through Portland he asked the manager at the Keith Theatre if he knew where I lived. "What do you want with him?" Jones replied, "Walter Smith told me that he has talent." So the manager gave him the wrong directions to get to my house and ran over [there] himself. He hadn't known that I could really play. When he got there he said, "I want to sign you up immediately to play for me every Sunday at the [Riverton] Amusement Park. I'll pay you $3.00 a concert." Just after I signed the contract, Jones arrived at my house. When he saw the manager coming out, he realized what had happened—but there was nothing that he could do about it. That was the first and last time that I ever came close to playing in a dance orchestra! If Jones had arrived first I probably would have taken the job. Money is money to a young kid. That's how close I came![19]

The Road to New York

The Wall Street crash in 1929 was a life-altering event for Vacchiano, just as it was for the rest of the country, In just one day, a record-breaking sixteen million shares of stock were traded with a total loss of thirty billion dollars. The aftermath of this devastation led to one of the greatest financial crises in the history of the United States, instantly ending a season of prosperity and ultimately ushering in the Great Depression. According to Vacchiano, "The day Wall Street crashed was to be the next milestone in my life. This was the beginning of the worst depression the country has ever witnessed, and it ultimately affected the entire world. The misery and suffering during these harsh years have been documented many times in novels, movies, plays, and certainly in history books."[20]

In the midst of this worldwide crisis, Vacchiano decided to pursue a two-year business course and obtain his license as a Certified Public Accountant (CPA) in order to maintain a stable income. The three leading business schools of the day were Bentley College (Boston), Wharton School of Business of the University of Pennsylvania (Philadelphia), and Saint John's University (Brooklyn). Vacchiano decided to visit Saint John's University first because his older sister, Anna, lived nearby. To Vacchiano's surprise and disappointment, Saint John's rejected his application because of the difference between Maine's grading system and the Regent's scale in New York.

Vacchiano decided to make the most out of his trip to New York and visit Times Square, a decision that changed his life forever.

> I remember they had just opened up the Radio City Music Hall in New York City, and there was a friend of mine from Portland, Oscar Jones, who was playing trumpet in the orchestra. I figured I had better go down and see Times Square—after all, you can't go to New York City and not go to Times Square. So when I was walking around the street in Times Square, I just happened to run into my friend from Portland. He asked what I was doing and I told him the whole story. He said, "While you're here, you must take one lesson from the great Max Schlossberg." I didn't know who he was. I said, "I certainly can't afford it." Jones then offered to lend me the $3.00 the lesson would cost.
>
> I made the appointment for Sunday morning and after the lesson I would take the bus to Boston. I was glad it happened that way, because I would be close to my home. Well, Schlossberg was very nice to me and after the lesson he said, "Vacchiano, you are very talented. I want you to stay here. I will give

11

you a full scholarship to the Institute of Musical Art." I figured I didn't have anything to lose and if I didn't make it after one year, I could always go back to Boston. So I told him, "Alright, I will stay."[21]

Max Schlossberg influenced Vacchiano's style and interpretation of orchestral playing more than any of his other teachers. This final ingredient of studying with Schlossberg created and solidified Vacchiano as a complete orchestral trumpet player, impacting the world of music for generations to come.

Max Schlossberg and The Juilliard School

Before discussing Vacchiano's lessons with Schlossberg, it is important to trace and examine Schlossberg's musical history. Schlossberg was born around 1873 in Libau, Latvia, which was part of Russia at that time. He attended the Imperial Conservatory in Moscow, where he studied with August Marquard, Franz Putkammer, and Adolph Souer. Schlossberg continued his training by moving to Berlin where he studied with Julius Kosleck, one of the most famous trumpet players in Europe. Kosleck was revered for his clarino style of playing that was unparalleled in Europe in the 1880s and 1890s.[22]

While in Berlin, Schlossberg had the privilege of touring with Arthur Nikisch, Felix Weingartner, and Hans Richter. After completing his studies in Berlin, Schlossberg then moved to Riga, Latvia, and played trumpet in the opera. In addition to trumpet, Schlossberg played the double-bass and was also a conductor.[23]

Schlossberg and his wife, Jennie Lehak, immigrated to America in 1903 to settle permanently in New York City. Not much is known about Schlossberg's career from 1903 until 1911, at which time he joined the New York Philharmonic as second trumpet. The thirty-two-week salary of the Philharmonic in 1911 was not enough to support a family, so Schlossberg also maintained a private studio of aspiring trumpet players and played in various chamber orchestras and theaters in the city.[24]

Schlossberg was appointed to the faculty at the Institute of Musical Art (IMA) in 1923, a position he held until his death in 1936. He taught only a small number of students at the IMA and they came to his apartment for lessons at 891 Tiffany Street in the East Bronx (later, between 1928–1930, he moved to 811 Walton Avenue in the West Bronx).[25] In addition to Vacchiano, other musicians such as Louis Davidson, Murray Karpilovsky, Manny Klein, Nathan "Nat" Prager, and James Smith also demonstrated Schlossberg's success as a trumpet teacher.

Vacchiano distinctly remembered his initial impression of the lessons with Schlossberg:

> I learned that the name Max Schlossberg was magic when I came to New York. The managers of all the orchestras, bands, and theaters would consult Schlossberg whenever they needed a replacement. When you walked into the room to study with him, you immediately felt like you were in the presence of a great man. He was very handsome and looked more like European royalty than a musician. He wore a fur-lined coat, walked with a cane, and had a waxed moustache with turned up corners.
>
> When I studied with him, he lived on Walton Avenue in the Bronx. His apartment was up on the top floor in the back and it was more or less soundproof. His studio walls were covered with pictures of all the famous trumpet players of the day, many of whom were his students. He would periodically point to them and tell you what desirable qualities each of them possessed; then he would say, "Pretty soon I'll have your picture up there!" He knew how to encourage a student and make him feel he was going to make it. Not once in my six years of affiliation did I ever hear him say an unkind word about anyone. He was above jealousy and never bragged about himself; he left that to others. He was a very kind man. I can't say enough about him.[26]

Weekly lessons with Schlossberg were built on a foundation of three main books: Arban's *Complete Method*,[27] Saint-Jacome's *Grand Method*,[28] and Sachse's *100 Studies*.[29] Drilling the student on these fundamentals was paramount to his teaching. He once told Vacchiano that practicing these rudiments of playing "is like pressing a pair of pants with a cold iron; you must go over it enough times to form a crease."[30]

Before Vacchiano came to New York, he had already completely gone through the Arban and Saint-Jacome methods with his previous teachers at least two or three separate times. When Schlossberg asked him if he had studied them, he said, "No" because he wanted to obtain Schlossberg's personal interpretation of these books. Vacchiano was a true student and wanted to acquire as much information as possible from such a masterful teacher.

In addition to these three method books, Schlossberg employed a style of teaching that was unique in the early years of the twentieth century. He frequently wrote out specific exercises designed for the individual student. For example, if a student had trouble with flexibility, Schlossberg composed an exercise specifically designed to train him to be more flexible. Years later, Harry Freistadt, the former first trumpeter with the CBS Orchestra and Schlossberg's son-in-law, compiled these drills into a book called *Daily Drills and Technical Studies for Trumpet*.[31]

Vacchiano explained how Schlossberg used these drills in his weekly lessons:

> He was a very slow and meticulous teacher. He would give you a little bit each week and continue to add to it. He had an exercise called "four-in-one" [fig. 1.1] where you played two octaves of a scale, two octaves of thirds, two octaves of chords and two octaves of intervals, all with one breath. It would take about three or four months to get that ability.[32]
>
> When you played for him it had to be right on the button. If he found a weakness in your playing, he would address it immediately and not move on until you could fix it. He would always tell me, "Practice your liabilities, not your assets."[33]

Schlossberg, Four-in-One, p. 37, #102a

Fig. 1.1

In addition to studying exercises from method books, Schlossberg discussed various compositions with Vacchiano and pointed out the importance of specific excerpts. He had Vacchiano write them out by hand to practice for his lessons. "One of the disadvantages of going to school in my time was the lack of music repertoire books. I used to spend hours at the library copying music by hand. The student today has the entire repertoire in conventional books at a nominal price. Every important selection is now available."[34]

Schlossberg not only educated his students in their technical abilities, but also instructed them on the intangible aspects of orchestral style and proper phrasing that enabled them to be complete musicians. The following story is a testament to Schlossberg's successful teaching:

> The reason Schlossberg was so great was his style. He put his stamp on you that was the stamp accepted by the finest orchestras.[35] What made him so famous is the instruction he got from Kosleck. He was a stylist and passed that on to Schlossberg. I witnessed this firsthand at the 1933 World's Fair in Chicago. My longtime friend from the Institute of Musical Art, Izzy Blank, and I hitchhiked to Chicago for the World's Fair. We went into a music store just pretending like we wanted to buy something. We actually just wanted to keep our lips up by trying out different trumpets.

So we were playing these trumpets and a well-dressed gentleman walked in and looked at me and said, "Oh, you are a very fine student of Max Schlossberg!" This was my first time to Chicago and this man had never seen me before. I was terrified and asked him, "How did you know I was a student of Schlossberg?" He said, "I recognize the style; the Max Schlossberg style. My name is Edward Llewellyn." This man was the greatest cornet soloist in America at the time! Schlossberg put an imprint on every student. This was because he had over one hundred rules of orchestral performance. The average student who didn't study with him wouldn't know anything about these rules. You had to get them from him. He had a rule for everything. It's not for any one specific piece of music, it's for everything in general. He was a great stylist.[36]

Vacchiano's years at the IMA yielded more than education; it was here that he met his wife-to-be, Ethel Josephine LaParde. Josephine, originally from Virginia, came to the IMA to continue her studies as a piano major and a clarinet minor. She was also very gifted in understanding music theory, and Vacchiano initially made her acquaintance while seeking additional coaching in his studies.[37] Eventually, this grew into a courtship, marriage, and the birth of two children, Ralph (1937–1976) and Jo Ann (1944–2011).[38]

Despite the economic state of the country, Vacchiano managed to earn a decent income playing in a variety of orchestras in the summer:

> Although the country was in the throes of a disastrous depression, I was being blessed with good fortune. The unemployment was so bad during the depression that President Roosevelt inaugurated the WPA (Work Project Act). Walter Damrosch, the dean of conductors and brother of Frank Damrosch (President and Founder of the Institute of Musical Art) formed an orchestra of 200 musicians. I remember we had sixteen trumpets, sixteen horns, and anyone with an instrument who wanted to earn twenty dollars.

That first winter we played all the Wagner operas at Madison Square Garden to an audience of 20,000. I don't know why, but [Damrosch] put me on first chair, even though there were other great players in the orchestra. I was so nervous and scared, but during the performance of *Rienzi* a prominent player from the Sousa Band came up to me and said, "Young man, you have started a new school of playing," and walked away.

On Saturday the Metropolitan Museum of Art was open house to the two symphony concerts led by David Mannes, Founder of the Mannes College of Music in New York. We rehearsed from 10:00 A.M. to 12:00 P.M. and then played two full concerts during the rest of the day—all for twenty dollars. We played to huge crowds since it was free. A ticket at any price was too much during those days.[39]

In addition to these valuable professional experiences, Vacchiano also had the opportunity to tour with the George Barrere Symphony and play principal trumpet at the Chautauqua Music Festival. While these experiences prepared him for the professional world, they were not enough to financially sustain him and his wife. As graduation came ever closer, he became increasingly concerned about his future.

A Dual Career as a Performer and Teacher

The Metropolitan Opera Orchestra and the New York Philharmonic each held auditions for a trumpet position on the same day.[40] The timing was perfect for Vacchiano because he had just begun his studies as a graduate student at Juilliard.[41] Vacchiano recounted one of the most important days of his life:

My big break came one day when the first trumpet of the Metropolitan Opera Orchestra, John Nappi, was to retire. Mr. Simone Mantia, the orchestra manager, auditioned me for the part. He knew me and my playing ability, so the audition was brief. He had me play just six notes from Strauss's *Der Rosenkava-*

lier [fig. 1.2], which called for a solid high C-sharp which is very difficult. I played it well and he gave me the position and wished me luck.

Strauss, *Der Rosenkavalier*, Trumpet in C

Fig. 1.2

That same day, a Monday, I had an appointment to audition for the New York Philharmonic Orchestra that was beyond my wildest dreams. Since I was invited to audition, it was only courteous that I show up at Carnegie Hall. There were only two applicants for the position, myself and Louis Davidson, unlike today where hundreds are appointed to apply for the position. I was auditioning for the great conductor Arturo Toscanini, and he asked me to play three notes from *La Mer* [fig. 1.3]. I played it well and was told to wait upstairs. After waiting, he called me down to play the same thing again, and also a third time. I was completely baffled at this point until the manager, Maurice Van Praag, told me this was considered a good test to see if I could play it three times in a row. When he told me I was now a member of the club, which meant I was engaged to play with the New York Philharmonic, I was thunder struck. I should have told him I was already engaged by the Metropolitan Opera, but I didn't dream I would get the position with the Philharmonic.

Debussy, *La Mer,* Cornet in C

pp *et très lointain*

Fig. 1.3

> I called up Mr. Mantia to see if he would release me. Mr. Mantia, who was one of the most loved men in the music business, said, "Vacchiano, that is a better job than this one. Take it and God bless you."
>
> I forgot to mention that just the night before, I'd been engaged to play in the pit of the new Broadway show by Cole Porter, *Anything Goes*! It's a good thing that didn't happen because I probably would have wound up a show player.[42]

Beginning in 1935, Vacchiano joined the New York Philharmonic as third trumpet (and assistant principal). The other members of the section were Harry Glantz (principal), Nat Prager (second), and Max Schlossberg (fourth). The first year for Vacchiano was incredibly surreal; he was playing with his musical mentors (Schlossberg and Glantz) and being conducted by some of the world's most famous musicians. Vacchiano recalled these early experiences:

> My first rehearsal was one that I will never forget. Toscanini was conducting Beethoven's *Symphony No. 4*. It's beyond my ability to describe my sensation and thrill. Playing under Toscanini and Bruno Walter was an incredible experience, but my greatest thrill was to play for a year with my old teacher, Max Schlossberg.[43]

During Vacchiano's first year with the Philharmonic, he was also appointed to the faculty at The Juilliard School.[44] The new teaching appointment filled out Vacchiano's weekly schedule while also giving him the opportunity to significantly increase his income. Vacchiano had an hour-and-a-half commute to rehearsals and had recently purchased a house in Flushing, New York, for $6,000 (the house he lived in until his death in 2005).[45] On Thursdays, Vacchiano had a large gap between the morning rehearsal and the evening concert, but the commute back home was too cumbersome. This gap was now easily filled with students at Juilliard. One year later, Vacchiano joined the faculties of the Manhattan School of Music and the Mannes College of Music.

As Vacchiano continued to develop a reputation for dependability, he began to play and record frequently all over the city. He estimated that during his career he recorded over 400 albums with various organizations, including the Columbia Orchestra (when they recorded in New York), Stokowski and His Orchestra, Kostelanetz and His Orchestra, Longines Symphonette, and the RCA Victor Symphony Orchestra.[46]

The popularity of radio broadcasts soon demanded more experienced orchestral players who could perform live with minimal rehearsal. Vacchiano described his involvement in this industry:

> There were three radio stations in New York that were able to broadcast nationally: NBC, CBS, and WOR. Each one had a permanent staff with a 52-week season. All the big corporations had specials every week. There were several symphonies that I took part in. On Monday night the Firestone 100-piece symphony played to a national hook-up. On Wednesday night the Celanese symphony performed. On Friday the WOR symphony broadcast a fine legitimate program. Sunday morning the Radio City Symphony Hall broadcast a full hour of standard works. A great many of these orchestras included many members from the New York Philharmonic. As symphonic players, we got first call on most of the classical work because we knew the repertoire and it saved money in rehearsal time. Sometimes there was a scheduling conflict, but the contractors used to arrange the rehearsals to suit many of the Philharmonic members. [It was a demanding job because] there was no si-

multaneous broadcast to the West Coast. If we played a show in New York at six o'clock, we might have to repeat it three hours later for the West Coast.[47]

By the 1940s, Vacchiano was in demand as both a performer and teacher to the extent that hopeful students had to wait over one year to get even one lesson with him. He used to say, "Make hay while the sun shines!"[48]—and he certainly did just that.

In the old days Prager and I used to play lots of outside jobs as a team. One time we were playing on 42nd Street and had only five minutes to get to Carnegie Hall. We got stuck in traffic and the orchestra played for five minutes before they even noticed that the trumpets weren't there! We came in while Toscanini was conducting Schumann's [*Symphony No.2*] and we missed the whole introduction.[49] Of course, he was furious with us. We did so many outside jobs that we used to have a police escort to take us from Liederkranz Hall to Carnegie on Sunday afternoons because we played from two until two-thirty and had to be up at Carnegie by three for the national broadcast.

We had to be in so many places at one time that we had people who made their livings just getting our instruments from one hall to the next and having cabs ready for us. There was a fellow named Tony who couldn't read or write, but he had a room with all of our instruments in it and he knew exactly which instrument was yours. He'd get it to your various jobs on time. We had a little quirk in those days. We had to have special people just to carry our instruments for us and get us sandwiches, as we'd never have time to eat. That's how busy we were.[50]

After World War II, Vacchiano experienced a tremendous influx of students due to the G.I. Bill. "I found myself teaching every spare hour in the week. As I look back I wonder how I did it, I taught as many as thirty hours a week in addition to my regular orchestral duties."[51]

However, an article from *The New York Times* in 1941 attests to the fact that Vacchiano's teaching skills were recognized by U. S. Army personnel during the war as well, and local efforts were made to train more trumpet players for military service.

The Philharmonic-Symphony Society of New York has a committee on musical training and scholarships which collects funds and then pays first desk men of the Philharmonic to train talented youngsters from the public schools in different instruments. Since last November about twenty-six of their graduates have been drafted. Those who played the trumpet have been welcomed by the Army with special warmth, and Army officials, having learned where the boys received their training, have flooded the committee with requests for more such expert trumpeters.

This gave Mrs. Harris R. Childs, the chairman, an idea. She and her friend, Mrs. Keyes Winter, have formed a special committee solely to raise funds to train more trumpeters for the Army. They are seeking $1,500 for the purpose and the young men will be prepared by William Vacchiano, one of the trumpeters of the Philharmonic.[52]

Vacchiano dealt with the increased load with earlier teaching times both at school and at home. Many private students recalled his teaching them on Saturday morning at 8:00 at the Juilliard building and sometimes on Sunday morning at his home in Flushing while still dressed in his bathrobe!

One might wonder why Vacchiano worked so much and never turned anything down. To explain this vigorous work ethic, he once commented:

I was a Depression child. When I came [to New York] it was the height of the Depression; everybody was terrified. You grabbed all you could. You never knew when things might go sour; you didn't turn anything down. Today, the salaries are great—we didn't have big salaries back then. Today, [some orchestras] pay thousands of dollars a year and you don't have to do all that extra work. The Philharmonic salary was seventy dollars a week when I first started and it was a twenty-eight-week season. When we played a concert there were so few people there you could go deer hunting and not hit anybody![53]

Having spent many years in the music business, Vacchiano witnessed the numerous fluctuations in job security and availability. He told all of his students, "The ideal situation for the musician today is the one with a university position where he can play solos, give quintet concerts, and play in a local orchestra."[54] To show his students the importance of having a degree, he went back to school to earn a bachelor's and master's degree in trumpet performance, both of which he completed at the Manhattan School of Music in 1952 and 1953, respectively.[55]

Along with the rewards of playing in the Philharmonic came the demands of playing under conductors who were notorious for their unrelenting pursuit of perfection. These demands, coming from the likes of Reiner, Rodziński, and Szell, increased the level of stress on each musician. Vacchiano relied on his deep religious convictions as he coped with the pressure of playing principal trumpet in the Philharmonic under many of the famous conductors in the world:

> I was very religious and that helped a lot. Most people, unfortunately, don't have that. They go in there and take their chances; I had somebody working for me! My mother instilled that in me and the whole family. When I was a boy, I had an accident and was thrown from a horse. The doctors told my mother that one leg would be shorter than the other. So she had a mass said for me in Rome and told me, "Let God take care of it."[56]

As the 1970s approached, Vacchiano began to realize the strain of playing in the Philharmonic for over thirty years. He had witnessed the physical ailments several of his colleagues acquired from playing under the pressure for too long and he decided it was time to retire while he was in good health. He had amassed a very full and rewarding career as principal trumpet in one of the world's greatest orchestras and he desired to retire while still in his prime.

Retirement Years (1973–2005)

After serving as principal trumpet with the Philharmonic for thirty-one years (1942–1973), Vacchiano retired from the principal desk, making history as the longest principal trumpet player of an American orchestra at the time of his retirement.[57]

Vacchiano described his reasons for retirement:

> Thirty-eight years with the Philharmonic was enough time—it was a tremendous strain. I was making more money on the outside anyway by teaching and playing radio dates. I was making fifty percent more and I didn't have to worry. I could now stay at home every night and relax. Most of these trumpet players when they retire, they don't retire at their peak. I wanted to retire at my peak. I played all around town, but I didn't have the strain. I didn't have to play *Zarathustra* on the broadcast. I began to take life easy by traveling with my wife and family; that is why I've lived so long.[58]

After retiring from the Philharmonic, Vacchiano filled up his newly found free time with teaching more students and traveling to neighboring states to give master classes. Eventually, he began compiling exercises into method and étude books for publication.[59] Each book was designed with a specific purpose in mind. In many instances, a particular student and the issues they worked on in lessons inspired the focus of the method books.

A prime example is the *Trumpet Routines* book he wrote for Phyllis Stork.[60] This particular book focuses on the rudiments of playing the trumpet, with each routine presenting all of the necessary fundamentals for the student to work through in a daily, methodical manner. Vacchiano stated in the foreword, "Most successful performers have set routines. This is the aim of these routines: the mastery of keys and the facility of technique. In order to reach your ultimate goal of perfection, you must concentrate on the requirements of a technique. Remember: Repetition is the mother of perfection."[61]

Aside from music, Vacchiano pursued several different pastimes throughout his career and retirement. One of these was his self-taught ability to read in five foreign languages: Italian, French, Spanish, German, and Portuguese.

> Reading in these foreign languages is a great hobby I enjoy. The way I learned them was by reading the Bible; I would place the English version on the left and the foreign version on the right. I would read a line first in English and then the foreign language; back and forth with no teacher. I can read Spanish like a native and I read the Spanish newspapers all the time. French was easy because I knew Italian; I actually read all of the Agatha Christie books in French. I also read Dante and similar authors in Italian. German was the most difficult, though.[62]

Vacchiano student, Richard Giangiulio, recognized this affinity for languages and reading:

> The locker in his lesson room at Juilliard was filled with books in foreign languages. If a student didn't show up, he would be in there reading all of these books in a variety of different languages. I found that very interesting because he was not only intellectual on the instrument, but he pursued those kinds of things to keep himself mentally active.[63]

A complement to his pursuit of languages was his interest in crossword puzzles and remarkable knowledge of historical facts. Dr. Philip Varriale, Vacchiano's doctor and former student, observed the following:

> As an avid reader, Bill was a wellspring of far-flung bits of information and became a vicarious contestant when he tuned in to his TV favorites—*Jeopardy* and *Wheel of Fortune.* As a fanatic for the crossword puzzle, Bill religiously worked the puzzle every morning including the *New York Times* puzzle every Sunday.[64]

One passion that is inherent among Italians is the love of food. His students were well aware of this, as David Krauss recalled:

> One of my favorite memories was when Brian Benson and I had Vacchiano over to our apartment one night for dinner. We

knew he loved Italian food, so we thought we would cook some lasagna. So he showed up at the door right on time with a six-pack of Miller Genuine Draft and we cooked the dinner. While we were sitting and chatting he said, "This is the best lasagna I have ever eaten." Of course we didn't believe him because we were just American kids cooking Italian food for him![65]

Vacchiano also had a special skill with numbers and mathematics. Even in his advanced years, he regularly kept his mind active by figuring the costs of various purchases like photocopies, groceries, airline flights, and gasoline—anything that would occupy his mind. This affinity with numbers is one reason why he almost became a CPA. I witnessed this myself when I was visiting Vacchiano one day to interview him and take a lesson. After spending a couple of hours with him, he gave me all his personal notes from master classes he had given over the years. He offered to walk to the photocopy shop with me to copy them. On the way he estimated it would be around twenty dollars to copy everything. After we finished and were walking out he asked how much it cost, and I said, "Seventeen dollars." He said, "Ah, that's not bad! That's pretty cheap!" Then he stopped outside the door and began mumbling. I finally realized he was figuring out how much each page cost! At ninety-two years of age he was still keeping his mind active every day.[66]

As Vacchiano got older, he began playing in numerous community bands just for fun. By the time he was in his nineties, his upper range was not very strong. He loved playing in the band so much he sometimes used an alto F trumpet to play the French horn parts. Many times he just sat and listened while enjoying the music. He was a quiet and humble man who remained dedicated to self-improvement even in this amateur environment, as his daughter, Jo Ann, stated:

> A few years ago he played third trumpet in a summer municipal band near our home. The trumpet section was seated on a riser and a step had to be made for my father so that he could get there. Apparently he was not pleased to have to use an extra step that none of the other trumpet players needed. To remedy

this he made a step with a railing the same height as the riser and practiced getting up on it all winter. The following summer he very proudly removed the extra step and went to his chair without any assistance! [67]

Even though Vacchiano began his semi-retirement in 1973, his contribution to the musical world did not go unnoticed. The International Trumpet Guild *Journal* (ITGJ) and the New York Brass Conference for Scholarships *Journal* (NYBCSJ) have published numerous articles in acknowledgment of Vacchiano's career as a performer and teacher.[68] Furthermore, the NYBCSJ gave him the Award of Recognition on January 22, 1978,[69] while also devoting an entire journal in honor of his many contributions to the music world. Similarly, the ITG gave Vacchiano the Honorary Award on June 5, 1984.[70] The most prestigious award Vacchiano received was an Honorary Doctorate from Juilliard on his ninety-first birthday, May 23, 2003.[71]

CHAPTER TWO

*V*ACCHIANO AND THE
NEW YORK PHILHARMONIC

✦

The New York Philharmonic

The New York Philharmonic, founded in 1842 under the leadership of Ureli Corelli Hill, is the oldest orchestra in continuous existence in the United States. Having performed over 15,000 concerts since its inception, the Philharmonic enjoys an immensely rich musical history. In 1882, the Philharmonic went on its first tour and since then has performed in 425 cities, 59 countries, and on 5 continents. It was one of the first orchestras to give a live radio performance (1922) and was the first to give a live coast-to-coast broadcast (1930). With nearly 2,000 albums to its name (with over 500 currently available), the Philharmonic is one of the most recorded orchestras in the world.[1]

During Vacchiano's membership with the Philharmonic, nearly every major conductor and soloist at that time visited the orchestra. The list of musical directors during his tenure includes Arturo Toscanini (1928–1936), John Barbirolli (1937–1942), Artur Rodziński (1943–1947), Bruno Walter (1947–1949), Leopold Stokowski (1949–1950), Dimitri Mitropoulos (1949–1958), Leonard Bernstein (1958–1969), George Szell (1969–1970), and Pierre Boulez (1971–1977). The exposure to these musical giants enriched not only Vacchiano's playing, but also his teaching. In lessons, Vacchiano frequently told students how to play specific excerpts to the liking of each individual conductor: "Bernstein likes this solo played this way, but Szell prefers it another way." This type of instruction was extremely rare, being offered by only a handful of other teachers in the country.[2]

Vacchiano's Perception of Various Conductors

Vacchiano viewed rehearsals as an opportunity to enhance his musical knowledge. He intensely watched the mannerisms and characteristics of every conductor. This necessary skill further proves the point that Vacchiano was always a student of music and the instrument. Even though he played many compositions several times, they were frequently performed with a variety of different conductors, especially over the course of thirty-eight years.

Vacchiano explained the diversity of interpretation between each conductor:

> To illustrate the effect of a conductor's personality on the interpretation of a composition, I'm reminded of an occasion when we had to play the *Star Spangled Banner*. During the war we opened every concert with it. Bruno Walter was conducting [the Philharmonic] one night when Koussevitzky and the Boston Symphony were appearing in town. At the same time, down at the Met, Pappe, the Italian, was conducting. When Koussevitzky led the anthem, he had in mind how Tchaikovsky might have felt it—very slowly. He really stretched it out. Bruno Walter thought of it as Wagner—in a brighter, more marcato approach. Pappe conducted it like *Rigoletto*—light and brisk. Toscanini was a rare case. He was the only Italian who was great with Wagner and Beethoven. He was better than the Germans with them.[3]

Even though each of these conductors had his own interpretation, an orchestra with the prestigious reputation of the New York Philharmonic had its own opinion of music:

The Philharmonic used to carry a lot of conductors. No matter what they did we'd always play—whether they knew the piece or not. No conductor can spoil Beethoven's *Fifth*. We had our own interpretation of it. In fact you'd have to be a pretty big man to change the orchestra's own impression of a piece. Very few conductors could do it. Usually by the end of the week, the conductor was doing it the way we wanted it done! But he didn't know it . . . he thought that it's all his idea.[4]

Vacchiano made the following comments regarding his observations of the diverse conductors who directed the Philharmonic:

On Toscanini:

My thirty-eight years of experience taught me all the ins-and-outs of all the conductors. Toscanini and Walter were the top two; they were the most important ones. Many of the others, like Szell, Rodziński, and Reiner were great, but they didn't have the soul of Toscanini and Walter. They were both refugees and they made music with such emotion; it was a thrill just to watch them. Toscanini was a ball of fire. He could explode instantaneously at the slightest provocation. Whenever he exploded, he had a reason. If you played well he would leave you alone and even show respect for you.[5]

Toscanini's habit of singing during rehearsals was the most unique thing I remember. He probably had the best ear in the music world, but he could not carry a tune. His form and grace on the podium were so beautiful to see that one almost forgot to listen to the music. His style was copied by every young aspiring musician. His face inspired us with admiration, respect, fear, and tension. When he made the great crescendo in *Pictures at an Exhibition* his face was really something to behold. The louder we played the redder his face would become.

Off stage he was an affable man who exuded charm and gentility. This was evident at the farewell dinner he gave us at the famous Astor Hotel. It was a party that was hard to forget.

He gave every man a brand new one hundred dollar bill, which was equivalent to two weeks salary, and a handful of Havana cigars, which were smoked by millionaires. The champagne flowed like water, not to mention the fine dinner itself. No other conductor showered such attention on the men. He moved from table to table spreading cheer and friendliness.[6]

On Walter:

Bruno Walter became the mainstay of the Philharmonic. All during the great depression the performances were always sold out, despite the hard financial times. His approach and attitude toward the men must have been like Haydn's contact with his men—a Papa Haydn image—a Papa Walter image.[7] Although Walter's temperament was outwardly calm and placid, his climaxes were astounding. I was one of his greatest admirers.[8]

On Bernstein:

One Sunday afternoon [November 14, 1973], Bruno Walter became ill right before our weekly national broadcast. We were performing Strauss's *Don Quixote*. Fortunately, we had a very talented young assistant conductor who jumped in without any notice whatsoever and caused a sensation. This young man was Leonard Bernstein. Bernstein did more for the Philharmonic than any other conductor in its long history. The orchestra was like a dormant giant that came to life under his baton. We recorded practically every program. Life under Bernstein was ideal. He was a humanitarian and musician all in one. He had talents that the other conductors didn't have. He was an excellent composer, a fine script writer, and a great public speaker.[9]

On Szell and Rodziński:

Rodziński and Szell were the same kind of conductor; they were what you call a "task-master"—very strict and dramatic. Szell basically ran the orchestra like it was an army. They didn't think so much like Toscanini and Walter. They didn't have the amount of feeling, but they were great conductors. Musically, they were very exact. Rodziński was hectic and disoriented much of the time and he had a nervous tick. He was highly neurotic and even carried a gun in his back pocket. His wife told all about this in her book, *Our Two Lives*.[10]

Vacchiano continued:

Every conductor has something they look for. Schlossberg taught me this early on; that is why he was so great. In Strauss's *Ein Heldenleben* [fig. 2.1], there is a lyrical trumpet solo at the end that has slurred sixteenth notes. Schlossberg taught me the sixteenths must be rushed to sound like thirty-second notes, otherwise they would sound like triplets. When I did that with Rodziński, he looked over and winked at me. I could tell he was waiting to tell me to do that beforehand.[11]

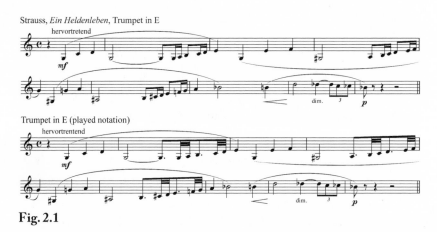

Fig. 2.1

On Mitropoulos:

Dimitri Mitropoulos hit the musical scene like a bolt of lightning. His debut in Boston was a great sensation and his success as a major conductor was instantaneous. His personality was the absolute opposite of Artur Rodziński. He wore a constant smile and seldom, if ever, lost his temper. Of all his assets, his memory was the most outstanding. He was the only conductor who ever came to rehearsals without a score. He had a habit of rubbing his forehead when thinking. We always said he was turning pages in his mind. He was a champion of ultra-modern music, which made his memory all the more remarkable. To memorize standard works is difficult enough, but to memorize avant-garde music is a real feat.[12]

The differences between Mitropoulos and Rodziński:

The contrast between Mitropoulos and Rodziński was also apparent in their approaches to ensemble. Mitropoulos's beat was free and lax. Great climaxes were his forte. He could raise an orchestra to great heights. Within an orchestra [that was] as routinized as the Philharmonic, we could contend with all types of downbeats and idiosyncrasies. Mitropoulos was very popular with the men because of his humbleness. He was plain and unpretentious. He lived very simply at the Great Northern Hotel down the street from Carnegie Hall and was completely unaffected in his daily life.[13]

On Reiner:

Some conductors were dramatic, while others were very precise. The best conductor was Reiner; his used a very small beat pattern and never wavered. They used to tell a joke about him. They say a fly landed on his baton and it stayed there for the whole concert—that is how small his beat was![14]

Vacchiano loved to tell interesting anecdotes about these famous conductors. One of his favorite stories was about Otto Klemperer:

This anecdote shows how great these men were, and yet naive. They didn't come down to earth as we do. Otto Klemperer had a very good friend named Mendelssohn. One day they went into Sam Goody's to buy Klemperer's version of Beethoven's *Eroica*. The young salesman thought he was a wise guy and said, "I don't have Klemperer, but I do have Bruno Walter's recording." Klemperer replied, "You don't understand, I am Klemperer and I want my own recording." The salesman didn't believe him and said, "And I suppose that's Beethoven standing over there." "No, that's Mendelssohn!"[15]

In addition to playing under these great masters, Vacchiano also had the privilege of premièring many significant compositions, sometimes with the composer at the helm. Such examples of world premières include Hindemith's *Symphonic Metamorphosis on Themes of C. M. Weber* (1944), Strauss's *Suite from "Der Rosenkavalier"* (1944), Stravinsky's *Symphony in Three Movements* (1946), Ives's *Symphony No. 2* (1951), and Copland's *Connotations for Orchestra* (1962). Other U.S. premières include Shostakovich's *Symphony No. 8, op. 65* (1944) and *Symphony No. 10, op. 93* (1954), Mahler's *Symphony No. 6* (1947), and Copland's *Symphony No. 2* (1957).[16]

The Philharmonic Trumpet Section

When Vacchiano joined the Philharmonic in 1935 as third trumpet (and assistant principal), Harry Glantz was principal, Nathan "Nat" Prager was second and Max Schlossberg was fourth. These three players were Vacchiano's idols as he was growing up and studying at the Institute of Musical Art; to play with them was a dream come true. Listening to Harry Glantz was an important part of Vacchiano's conception of sound and style:

> While studying at Juilliard, I used to listen to a record of Harry Glantz playing the *Coronation March* by Meyerbeer with Mengelberg conducting. I almost wore this recording out because I played it so much! He had a fantastic orchestral sound and I just wanted to get that *sound* in my ear. Sitting next to him for seven years was a great education for me.[17]

After sitting in such a solid section for seven years, Vacchiano was primed for taking over the reins as principal trumpet. Bruno Walter appointed him to principal trumpet in 1942.

> It all happened very suddenly. We were doing a recording down in the Liederkranz Hall on Monday afternoon, [May 4]. We were playing Gershwin's *Piano Concerto in F*. Glantz, who was already playing with the NBC Symphony, was there and when the set was over, he told the manager, "I am quitting." He came

over to me and said, "You're the first trumpet player now." Just like that, within five minutes I was the new principal. I had to go see Bruno Walter and he confirmed my new position.[18]

By 1948, the trumpet section had settled in with Vacchiano (principal), Nat Prager (second), John Ware (third/assistant principal) and James Smith (fourth). Each man had a unique skill in addition to his typical duties.

> My second trumpet player, Nat Prager, was fabulous. He was one of the best trumpet players in the country. He could do things no one else could do and saved my skin a lot of times. When I needed him he was really there. Johnny Ware was very good because he never got lost. Sometimes I would get rattled in these modern pieces—it's hard to look at the conductor and the music. Johnny knew exactly where we were all the time. If he wanted to be principal trumpet, I would've been out of a job! Jimmy Smith and I were actually classmates at the Institute. I brought him in because he had a fantastic low register. I needed somebody on fourth trumpet like that. He used to really pump out the low notes.[19]

Vacchiano and Nat Prager

Special mention needs to be given to the unsung hero Nat Prager, who was second trumpet from 1929 to 1963. Prager is one of the most under-recognized trumpet players of the twentieth century. Vacchiano describes his musical prowess:

> He had the greatest technique, the greatest embouchure. Even the great soloists couldn't come close to him as far as technique, speed, and everything else was concerned. He was outstanding! He was a great, humble gentleman. We all loved him. He was fabulous. Everybody recognized Prager. There was never any question as to who was the best. He walked away with all the prizes.[20]

Prager added an interesting element to the section because he *al-* *ways* played everything on B-flat trumpet. Mike Hipps witnessed this on one occasion:

> I remember them doing the Bach *Magnificat* with Bernstein. Vacchiano was playing first on an F trumpet, Prager was on second with a B-flat (he never played anything but a B-flat), and Johnny Ware was playing third on a D trumpet. Amazingly, they all matched with a perfect balance and blend.[21]

The Philharmonic trumpet section was unique during Vacchiano's tenure. All of them were working a substantial number of gigs outside of the Philharmonic and Vacchiano was the busiest of them all. Because of the pressure and demands placed on him both in the orchestra and in the studio, Vacchiano often used the other members of his section to assist in various ways. Frank Kaderabek, a student of Prager's, recalled the following story:

> I can remember seeing Vacchiano play many concerts when he had the flu or when he was really sick and it was a struggle. Yet, he had guys with him like John Ware and Nat Prager. I remember even John Ware telling me that Bill would lean over and say, "Nat, I'm sick, can you play this high C for me?" Nat would lean over and, BING, nail that high C and that's the way they worked. I feel like that trumpet section was the most incredible section because they worked like a team. They got along like a team, too. Bill was never a *prima donna*. I can remember many, many times Nat Prager saying to me, "Gee, didn't Bill sound great on this or that?" Prager never looked for the spotlight on himself. It was a great tribute to a great trumpet section because they did things that nobody else could do.[22]

A demonstration of this teamwork was captured on videotape during a *Young People's Concert* while they were playing Stravinsky's *Petrouchka*.[23] During the "Ballerina's Dance," Vacchiano had Prager play a handful of notes so he could regain his breath. While listening to just the audio portion of this recording, it is impossible to determine where Vacchiano stops and Prager begins.

Manny Laureano gives an account of the scene:

> Vacchiano used Nat Prager a tremendous amount. It had more to do with just the sheer amount of playing that he did outside of the orchestra. When these guys played rehearsals and concerts with the Philharmonic, they were shot half the time from doing all the recording sessions and so forth. Vacchiano used an assistant because he had the greatest assistant in Nat Prager. Nat was phenomenal. He would do things that were just seamless. The *Petrouchka* from the Bernstein video is a good example, too. You could see him gearing up mentally. It was just in his brain—he became Vacchiano a few measures before and is him while he is playing, then he releases it. Just incredible![24]

Prager's one flaw was that he got uncontrollably nervous if he had to play any part with "first trumpet" printed on it. His colleagues sometimes tricked him by scratching out "first" and writing in "second" just to see if he could do it. This phenomenon has been confirmed by numerous students, colleagues, and family:

> Prager could play anything you put in front of him as long as it said second trumpet. I once did a TV show with him and we spent a lot of time just sitting around and doing nothing. During that time, Prager played through probably more than half of Smith's *Top Tone* book from memory. He was sitting there with his legs crossed and pipe in one hand—it was just scary.[25]

According to Prager's daughter, Eileen Prager Perry, "His nervousness was primarily part of his personality. It seems to be somewhat of a Prager trait. My cousin, Cathy Prager, and I often joke about that—'expect the worst, hope for the best.'"

Another factor that contributed to Prager's stigma about playing first trumpet was an injury to his lip at an early age. As a youngster of nine or ten, he played an abundance of Jewish gigs and many long hours for the silent movies. After several years of this demanding playing, he developed a callous on his lip that was ultimately corrected through surgery. Even though the surgery was successful, he was always very cautious of his endurance and rarely practiced more than what was absolutely necessary.[26]

Prager's reluctance to play first trumpet was so well known among the music community that composer Julius Levine composed a piece for him called, "Timid Tim, The Trumpeter."[27] This piece, performed by the Philharmonic on a *Young People's Concert* on October 20, 1951, featured the second trumpet.[28] Prager was backed into a corner to play a solo, but since it was written for "second trumpet" he had no problems.

John Ware, who was Vacchiano's second-longest colleague in the trumpet section, summed up his experience as a member of one of the greatest orchestral trumpet sections:[29]

> In all [the] years that I [was with] the Philharmonic, only twenty-five years were spent with Bill. In my opinion, that time with Bill and Nat Prager on second trumpet were to me the finest section that ever existed in this country, and I'm including my position as third trumpet. I mean Bill and Nat Prager played a better first and second trumpet in a symphonic orchestra than anyone before and I think it will never happen again. They had a special rapport and quality between them. That quality of information will never be duplicated.[30]

Sadly, Nat Prager died from a heart attack at the age of fifty-three in 1963.[31] When Vacchiano received news of this tragedy, he said, "It felt as if someone had cut off my right arm," indicating how close the two had become during their twenty-eight years as colleagues in the Philharmonic. Prager left some large shoes to be filled and Vacchiano called on one of his former students to fill them, Carmine Fornarotto.

His daughter, who was only seven years old, related the story of that tragic evening:

> A few years ago I had a chance to visit with Lewis Van Haney, the trombone player from the Philharmonic, because he retired

near Tucson where I live. He asked a mutual friend of ours if he could meet me because he and my father had been best buddies. He told me that on the day my father died he was clutching his chest and not feeling well at rehearsal. A couple of the guys said, "Look, Nat, don't take the bus back to Jersey. Stay here and we'll get the car and swing around and pick you up." By the time they had come back to get him, he had already gotten on the bus.

When he got home, he ran his usual errands in town. My mother said it was almost like he was trying to prove to himself that he was okay because he took the car that *didn't* have the power steering. When he got home, I noticed he would put his hand on his chest every once in a while. I was seven years old at the time and I can still remember asking him, "Daddy, are you okay?" and he said, "Yeah, I just don't feel well—I'm kinda tired." Then I kissed him goodnight.

My brother's bedroom was just across the hallway from my parents' room, and we heard some commotion coming from in there. When we went in, my mother was trying to help him regain consciousness. He was sitting on the edge of the bed, but instead of falling with his head to the pillow, he fell straight back and then I remember her saying to my brother, "Get Eileen out of here!" By the time the paramedics came he was dead. It all happened very quickly.

I don't have a lot of memories from when I was seven, but that night I remember very vividly. My mother was unbelievable and she kept everything the same for us. My father died May 1st and that June he had planned a family trip to go to Washington D.C. She took us as planned because she didn't want anything disrupting our lives. She never remarried and she supported our family on a teacher's salary. She was an incredible role model and always talked about him. They fell in love when she was just sixteen.[32]

Prager left an indelible impression as a loving and humble man on all of those he knew. For the next thirty or forty years, Johnny Ware took flowers to his gravesite in loving memory. Prager's influence touched Leonard Bernstein to the extent that he set up a special fund to help pay for Prager's two children to go to college.

Years after my father's passing, Bernstein was guest conducting with the Philharmonic and Vladimir Ashkenazy was playing one of Prokofiev's piano concertos and Johnny Ware took me in so I could sit in the audience to listen. At the break, there was a line going down Philharmonic Hall to see Mr. Bernstein. I wasn't about to get in that line. I figured I'd tell my mother I couldn't see him. Just about then Johnny Ware came down to the front of the stage and waved me up. As I walked passed all these people, he said, "Bernstein doesn't want to see anybody but you." He truly admired my parents, and it was a real honor that he wanted to see me. He spent his whole break with me. He asked about my mom, my education, and how I was doing in school. I told him I was a musician and played the piano. We kept in touch with him for a long time and he always sent us holiday cards.[33]

Personal Impressions of
Vacchiano's Musicianship[34]

To better understand Vacchiano's musical personality, it is best to see him through the eyes of those who were closest to him. The following quotations are from various colleagues and students who sat next to him in the Philharmonic, persevered through weekly lessons, or regularly observed live performances.

Ranier De Intinis describes Vacchiano's leadership in the brass section:

> When I first joined the orchestra, the principal brass players were Vacchiano, Gordon Pulis (trombone), and James Cham-

bers (horn). Everything they did—intonation, rhythm, articulation, timbre, and dynamics—was right where it needed to be all
the time; there was never any question. Bernstein used to say,
"This is a push-button brass section. All you have to do is push
the button and they play it the way you want."[35]

Frank Kaderabek on the Vacchiano-Prager teamwork:

I saw a concert once of the Philharmonic where they played
Petrouchka. When they got to the "Ballerina's Dance," Bill
played the articulated sections and Nat Prager (second trumpet) played the slurred parts; they traded off through the whole
solo. I sat there staring from the balcony of Carnegie Hall with
my mouth wide open. I couldn't believe what I was seeing and
hearing because it sounded like one guy. I had also seen Bill
play *Petrouchka* on other occasions when he played the whole
thing like it was no sweat. They did things like that all the time;
it was just part of the job.[36]

Adel Sanchez on Vacchiano's lyrical abilities:

One wonderful experience I had was the first time I ever heard
Vacchiano play live; he played Copland's *Quiet City* and he
played it on his D trumpet. His lyrical playing was outstanding;
he made it sound like the trumpet had no valves. He had this
incredibly liquid sound. I asked him in my next lesson, "How
did you do that?" He kind of smiled and said, "Does Macy's tell
Gimbels?" He never did tell me![37]

Mike Hipps describes the passion in Vacchiano's playing:

I distinctly remember hearing a concert where the Philharmonic was playing Ernest Chausson's *Symphony in B-flat*, which has
a lot of lyrical passages for trumpet. The solos he played were so
passionate and beautiful that they brought tears to my eyes.[38]

Hipps on Vacchiano's powerful high notes:

There was one week when I heard two performances of *Zarathustra*. The first one was with Ormandy and the Philadelphia
Orchestra with Gil Johnson playing principal. The second one

was later in the week with the Philharmonic and Karl Böhm conducting and the contrast between the two was really interesting. The opening with Philadelphia was beautiful and well balanced, with a wonderful, warm sound that never got out of control. When the Philharmonic did it, it just shocked you. Vacchiano would start that high C with the horn down, and then he would bring it up and the whole orchestra would come with him—he could lead the whole orchestra and it was just thrilling.[39]

Robert Karon on Vacchiano's musical personality:

I went to a concert and they were playing Gershwin's *An American in Paris* and he picked up his C trumpet for the solo and you have never heard it played like that. His sound went out over the whole orchestra and it was a dream. It had so much character to it; rich with personality and tone color. Every note had a meaning. For that moment, he was bigger than life.[40]

Manny Laureano tells about the revelation of hearing Vacchiano for the first time:

Interestingly, my first encounter with Mr. Vacchiano wasn't a lesson; it was when I was a senior in high school. I was a member of the all-city high school orchestra and we were playing a joint concert with the Philharmonic. During one of the rehearsals I got to hear Copland's "Buckaroo's Holiday" from *Rodeo*. I can still hear him playing that wonderful extended solo in the middle ("If he'd be a buckaroo by his trade"); I had never heard a sound produced quite like that. It was the first time I had ever heard his famous vibrato, articulation and everything that he did; it was a revelation.[41]

Malcolm McNab on the immensity of Vacchiano's sound and strength:

I had the pleasure one time of playing with Vacchiano on stage. The West Point Band played a concert where we sat behind the orchestra and we played Berlioz's *Symphony Funeral and Triumphant*. When the march begins, the band joins the orchestra. William Steinberg was conducting and we were all sitting there in our band uniforms. We could only see the heads of the brass section that were several rows in front of us. Vacchiano was resting during one of the tutti parts in the march where the band and orchestra were playing together. I will always remember that the instant he brought his horn up and started to play, the volume of sound in the hall doubled! He was the only one who had not been playing![42]

Al Ligotti tells how Vacchiano stood up for the players in his section:

One of my first times I played extra with the Philharmonic, Bernstein was the conductor. An associate conductor led the morning rehearsal, and Bernstein came in after lunch. It was a piece by Varèse, and Bernstein said, "Let's start at this letter," which was in the middle of the piece where the fifth trumpet—me—starts the passage up to the first part. Somebody said, "Why are you going to start there?" Bernstein said, "I want to start there." Just then Bill spoke up and said, "What are you gonna start there for, Lenny, are you trying to put somebody on the spot?" He said, "No, I want that spot; I am the conductor." So all the players in the section bent down below the stand and they played twice as loud with me so if I got nervous you wouldn't hear it—it was marked *fff.* That was the only time Bernstein ever came after me, and Vacchiano went right to bat. He was very protective. I talked to him about it afterward and he said, "Look, if you weren't good enough, you wouldn't be sitting here. Bernstein just has to trust me. That's my job." Bernstein never called anyone out to play alone, but for some reason he saw a new face back there and he decided to check me out. He never bothered me again. Vacchiano always protected his section and students.[43]

Fred Mills presents a picture of the pressures and demands over which Vacchiano prevailed:

One remarkable experience that I remember was when Mr. Vacchiano invited me to come to a Monday night CBS recording session when he was soloist in the Shostakovich *Piano Concerto, op. 35* with the Philharmonic. Bernstein was conducting while André Previn was the piano soloist. Mr. Vacchiano was unbelievably fine, even after recording Nielsen's *Symphony No. 5* all afternoon. His powerful endurance didn't wane after playing for over six hours while he continued to spin that beautiful Vacchiano sound through the cadenza in the Shostakovich first movement. The recording is still around and the ending is spectacular.[44]

Louis Ranger reveals one of his favorite Vacchiano recordings:

There's a very important recording of Bill in his prime playing Berg's *Wozzeck* with Mitropoulos conducting. Bill sounded absolutely magnificent on that record. This was also at a time when most orchestral players would have looked at that music as something from outer space. All of those impossible licks are clean and brilliant; despite their treacherous character, it was quite miraculous. It was a real lesson in how not only to play literature many people considered off the beaten path, but to play it beautifully.[45]

Abe Katz illustrates Vacchiano's seriousness during rehearsals:

I first came into contact with Bill at Juilliard. [At that time] it was Bill Vacchiano, Izzy Blank, Jimmy Smith, and myself in the section. I was accustomed to counting bars [of rest] . . . and I noticed that the other fellows never used to bother counting. And I said, "Fellows, don't you ever count?" One of the guys said, "You don't have to count. Just watch Bill Vacchiano." "What the hell does watching Bill have to do with counting?" Well, ten bars before our entrance, this is what he does. (Katz raises a trumpet and with exaggerated motions places the mouthpiece on his forehead and slowly brings it down over his nose, down to his upper lip and finally settling on his embouchure.) Sometimes twelve bars. Don't go away. And on the downbeat of the tenth bar we all came in. Well, I was glad. It saved us all a lot of wear and tear. Bill was always reliable.[46]

Stephen Chenette's impression upon his first hearing of Vacchiano's playing:

I was sixteen years old when I heard the Philharmonic for the first time. They were performing in Carnegie Hall and when Mr. Vacchiano started playing I looked at the brass section to find the trumpeter who was playing in unison with him. I just couldn't believe that any one person could get a sound that rich. I still think that he had the most beautiful trumpet sound that I have ever heard. I told him this the last time that I saw him (at the 2000 ITG Conference in Purchase, NY) and he replied, in a wistful voice, "I wish I still had it."[47]

Irwin Katz describes Vacchiano's legacy:

Vacchiano impacted the brass community by establishing a sound and style of playing that has brought us to where we are today. His playing style was always with a big and very lyrical bravura sound. You always knew when Vacchiano was playing. Regarding his pedagogy, he was a pioneer and a student of the instrument. He was always asking himself, "How can I do this better?"[48]

Olin Downes, a music critic for *The New York Times*, comments on a live performance of Bach's *Brandenburg Concerto No. 2*:

True, [the *Brandenburg Concerto No. 2*] must be played with a sure virtuosity on the part of the soloists, including the player of the high trumpet who "highly" distinguished himself last night. The performances were of an exhilarating mastery. It is hard to imagine interpretation more thoroughly in the charac-ter of the music. . . . The trumpeter, Mr. Vacchiano, sat behind his music sheet while he performed deeds of daring-do with a prevailing virtuosity and spirit that communicated a breathless excitement. Would he, could he, keep it going, way up there in the stratosphere? . . . What he [accomplished] with the pealing, silvery tones of his instrument was one of the features of the evening to remember.[49]

Chandler Goetting on Vacchiano's tone quality:

I will always remember Vacchiano's tone. It wasn't dark; it was bright, shiny, and coppery. It matched perfectly with James Chambers on horn; it had a core. The primary thing I took from Vacchiano was his concept of tone. I have always tried to sound like that.[50]

Gerard Schwarz on the personality of Vacchiano's playing:

The thing about Vacchiano was that he had a tremendous personality as a player. That was the real key. You heard him play three notes and everybody knew who it was. It was an incredible sound with distinct personality.[51]

Frank Hosticka gives a representation of Vacchiano's unique sound:

Vacchiano had an extremely haunting sound that was full of many colors. He could really float a note out with no sense of power or energy—it would just be there. It was a very distinctive and very beautiful musical sound. He learned to play with a certain lightness of approach even though he was an orchestral player. His sound was his most unique quality. Just listen to the Mahler recordings with Bruno Walter—the solos are haunting and his interpretations are immaculately impeccable.[52]

Charlie Schlueter tells about the personal sacrifices he made to hear Vacchiano play with the Philharmonic:

There were many times when I would skip a meal so I could afford to go to a concert. Hearing Mr. Vacchiano in the New York Philharmonic every week was an integral part of my studying with him. He rarely played in my lessons, so to hear him in Carnegie Hall week after week was a fantastic experience. His sound was glorious to hear: it had so much presence; it sort of reached out and touched you. I learned first-hand what he meant about rhythm, tone, phrasing, style, power, subtlety, and everything else he emphasized in lessons.[53]

Edward Treutel gives evidence of Vacchiano's tenacity and dedication to practicing:

> Max Schlossberg, our teacher, frequently evoked the names Blank, Davidson, and Vacchiano to inspire the rest of us to higher achievements. I well remember walking [Vacchiano's] wife Jo, a fine clarinetist, home after rehearsals and sitting in their apartment while Bill practiced on and on. The country was in the midst of a severe depression—it was difficult to support one's self and life was competitive. The craze seemed to be to practice more than anyone else and sitting there hearing him practice would make me uneasy about my own practice schedule. Bill was then, and has remained, a conscientious and devoted student of the trumpet.[54]

Abe Katz also attests to Vacchiano's practice habits:

> My earliest impression of Bill was his complete and deadly serious dedication to the horn. At Juilliard, when the brass section was temporarily excused, we would usually hang around, admire the girls, or whatever. Not Bill. He would invariably seclude himself in one of the practice rooms and do just that. Practice! Practice! Practice! Can you believe anyone visiting a dentist, going into the living room and practicing until his appointed time? I know, because that dentist was my father. My mother couldn't believe such a sound could come out of a horn.[55]

Bob Johnson, former horn player with the Philharmonic, comments on the versatility of Vacchiano's playing:

> He was also a master of all the idioms. For example, Randall Thompson's *Second Symphony* has a jazzy element to it. Bill's sound was still symphonic, but it had the requisite buoyancy to it that made it fun and exciting. When Bill played even the simplest theme—as in a Strauss waltz—he made the whole orchestra sound as if it belonged there doing just that music, as

if it had been there since eternity. He was about as versatile as anybody could be. You really wanted to dance with him when you heard him play in these various roles.[56]

CHAPTER THREE

ESPONSIBILITIES OF A
PRINCIPAL TRUMPETER

✦

Principles of Orchestral Musicianship

In the context of sight-reading and transposition, Vacchiano taught
many rules of orchestral style. Vacchiano absorbed these rules from
his lessons with Schlossberg, as well as from his exposure to the great
conductors who came through New York. Vacchiano performed under
them all so many times that he knew how to play every major trumpet
solo to their individual taste.

These rules were not hard-and-fast, but rather a starting point for
interpreting orchestral music. Vacchiano made it very clear that Mozart
was played differently from Wagner and that Strauss was played differently from Bruckner. The Italian style differs vastly from the French
style, which is different from the German style. The rules address how
to play each style appropriately in terms of rhythm, phrasing, articulation, sound, and dynamics. Vacchiano taught the rules in a general sense
rather than as individual rules pertaining to specific compositions. This
instruction enabled students to collect the necessary tools to correctly
perform compositions with which they were unfamiliar. If studied and
applied correctly, this knowledge is sufficient to govern the appropriate
style of virtually every composition.[1]

To emphasize how fundamental these rules are to orchestral performance, Jeffrey Silberschlag refers to the following story:

> On my first day as principal trumpet of the Italian National Symphony, I was consciously playing with the Vacchiano orchestral rules in mind when the second trumpet player leaned over to the French horn player and said in Italian, "Everything is going to be fine, this guy knows the rules." I was completely across the Atlantic Ocean and the rules still applied even though I could barely speak Italian.[2]

Stephen Chenette made this observation about Vacchiano's concept of sound and style:

> Vacchiano not only had an incredible ear for transposition and solfège, but also for subtle nuances of sound. In the lessons, while various experimentations of mouthpieces and trumpets occurred, he would intently listen for the timbre and sound that would be most desirable in an orchestra. The absolute best thing about his teaching was his ear. He could listen to you play on a number of different mouthpieces and trumpets and he could say which one was better and why. Also, if you played a passage in two different styles, he could tell you which way was preferable. His lessons educated your ear, so that after a while you could recognize the proper qualities of sound, style, and nuance. He pointed your mental conception in the right direction. No one could do this as well as Vacchiano.[3]

Thomas Stevens gives a personal testament to the pervasiveness of these rules in the music world:

> The rules Vacchiano enforced with me were about the rudiments of music, i.e. melodic cadences (internal, half, full, cadential extensions and so on) and the rhythmic figure placement rules, think two at a time but play the written ligatures . . . groups of 4-6-8, etc. Indeed, when personally witnessing master classes by such musical luminaries as flutist Marcel Moyse, oboist Marcel Tabuteau, et al., I was astonished by how

similar the teaching was to Vacchiano's (which even included the use of much of the same terminology).[4]

Phyllis Stork describes how thoroughly Vacchiano knew the rules and general rudiments of playing:

> Vacchiano once told me that he never made a mistake in the orchestra. What he meant was that his understanding of music and chord structure was amazingly well engrained. Even if he didn't play the written note, it would still be a right note because it was part of the chord structure. He might not have played the written note, but it all worked out because it was in his fingers and his ear.[5]

Vacchiano on Orchestral Excerpts

Even though Vacchiano's approach to teaching was rooted in fundamentals, he still spent a significant amount of time covering the orchestral literature. This was a vital part of his teaching because of his vast experience with the Philharmonic. This two-pronged pedagogical approach of fusing fundamentals with orchestral literature enabled Vacchiano's students to be well rounded and successful in a variety of musical settings, preparing them for the demands and pressures of the music world.

Vacchiano invariably came across a student who was very bull-headed and overly confident in his abilities. Vacchiano thoroughly enjoyed interacting with this type of student and keeping a tight leash on his ego. When he encountered a combative attitude, his response was something similar to:

> My knowledge of the repertoire is undisputable because I have recorded almost everything under the greatest master conductors. Who can dispute Bruno Walter's Mahler or Stokowski's Bach? I played all the Stravinsky compositions with the composer at the helm. Everything I teach is first-hand information, not hearsay. If you don't agree with me, here is the recording— you can argue with it![6]

Vacchiano stressed the point that he had learned from the best teachers and performed under the most respected conductors. He also realized the importance of heeding instruction from a master teacher. In teaching these excerpts, Vacchiano was extremely particular and would not allow for any error, no matter how small or seemingly insignificant. His teaching in this arena was complete, comprising a strong foundation of fundamentals, sensitivity to style, musical nuance, and historical background. This instruction taught the student not only how to play correctly and efficiently, but also how to dissect and develop his or her own playing.

Historical Background of Compositions

The historical background of musical compositions is extremely important for interpretation and style. Being principal trumpet of one of the pre-eminent orchestras in the world, Vacchiano had the opportunity to perform under legendary conductors such as Bruno Walter (Mahler's personal assistant), as well as première many works by Hindemith, Stravinsky, Schoenberg, Copland, and Bernstein.[7] While performing these selections with the composer conducting, Vacchiano was exposed to the first-hand accounts of the background and interpretation desired by the composer.

Bruno Walter was one of Vacchiano's largest influences regarding the background and interpretation of the Mahler symphonies. From 1901 to 1912, Walter was Mahler's personal assistant in Vienna. After Mahler's death, Walter gave the première performances of his mentor's *Das Lied von der Erde* and the *Symphony No. 9*. Vacchiano explains this influence on the recordings he did with Walter:

> There are many stories to Mahler's music and I know them all. Bruno Walter passed them on to me and he always wanted me to play with them in mind. If you listen to the recording of Mahler's *Symphony No. 1*, you'll notice a lot of different things I do because of what he told me. Walter said, "[In the third

movement there is] a five piece band in a small village. One man is a farmer and one man is a laborer, but there are only five players in the band and none is a professional. You realize that these men never practiced, so if they get a chance to make a few dollars playing for a funeral, they leave their businesses and get together. Mahler is trying to depict this type of bad playing, and you must play it poorly. Now, after the funeral, the band is going from the cemetery back home. So, they start to jazz it up and play fast. That's the fast section of the piece. When they get into the village they slow down again to show the people that they're somber. Then, when they leave the village again, it gets fast." All this knowledge helps you to play more effectively and passionately.[8]

This pervasive chain of verbal instruction is important when tracing and understanding its ongoing significance. Frank Hosticka relates the following story while he was playing with the Met:

Bruno Walter was a magnificent conductor. One of his protégés was George Szell and one of Szell's students was James Levine. Years later, Levine was doing concerts with the Met and he tackled a Mahler symphony. I swear to you, he started teaching the orchestra how to play this piece and I heard Bill Vacchiano's verbiage coming out: this eighth-note, this sixteenth-note, and story after story. It was like seeing the whole cycle completed. It is probably a very nineteenth-century concept, this whole idea of orchestral style, but this is what Vacchiano really understood and this is what he taught.[9]

Vacchiano cited Beethoven's *Leonore Overture Nos. 2 and 3* as specific examples of the importance of the musical background:

If you know you are saving a man's life with the bugle call, you'll approach the whole thing differently. This man is in a dungeon; his life depends upon that trumpet. If you pick up the horn and play it like a serenade, it's not good. You have to come in there with a strong blast. When you play that call somebody shoots a pistol at the same time to arouse the audience and give them an extra thrill. Now if you know all these stories it is wonderful and will add to the excitement of performance for both you and the audience.[10]

In addition to the historical context of compositions, it is important to understand a variety of interpretations, especially regarding tempo. Walter brought one such example to Vacchiano's attention while on tour:

> I remember that Bruno Walter called me into his stateroom when we were crossing the ocean the first time we went to Edinburgh. He said: "Remember, we have to play things a little slower in Europe than we do in America. Here, some people have to worry about making the subway, they have to get home, whereas over there they don't have to worry about time." All the compositions were about five minutes longer there.[11]

Approach to Specific Styles and Excerpts

In Vacchiano's teaching of orchestral excerpts, he had very specific ideas of how each excerpt was to be played, oftentimes including small tricks making them easier to play. On one occasion, he made the mistake of omitting some notes that were absolutely crucial:

> At a very early age I learned my lesson the hard way of knowing when to play and when not to play. The first summer I played in the Chautauqua Symphony we played the "Hallelujah Chorus" from Handel's *Messiah*. My friend and I decided to play it safe and lay out during the four-note descending scale in the middle. We didn't know it was a big solo! After experiencing that embarrassment, we played everything unless we had played the piece before.[12]

One of the difficulties plaguing many trumpet players in the orchestra is the unavoidable challenge of playing a solo after a long period of rest. A prime example is the octave jump from C_5 to C_6 in Strauss's *Also Sprach Zarathustra*. Several measures before the trumpet enters the orchestra is playing at full force. The foolproof trick Vacchiano used was to stick a mute in and play the octave jump during the orchestra's tutti section to prepare his lip for the solo. The orchestra was loud enough that the muted trumpet could not be heard. He then took his mute out and played the actual written part. "My lips would be tingling from the abuse, but the good thing is I didn't have to come in cold. If I didn't follow this procedure, I would have to play on a cold lip with varying results."[13]

The bugle call to Beethoven's *Leonore Overture Nos. 2 and 3* (fig. 3.1) requires the off-stage trumpet to come in at a very precise moment. Vacchiano devised a plan to ensure the preciseness of this entrance. He memorized the orchestral melody leading up to the bugle call and played along with the orchestra from backstage, so that when the orchestra stopped he was ready to come in without any gap. "Invariably, the conductor would say, 'How did you know to come in at such an exact time?' I never told them my secret. You always hear a break between the trumpet and the orchestra because the trumpeter doesn't know these things. He who hesitates is lost!"[14]

Beethoven, *Overture to "Leonore" No. 2*, Trumpet in E-flat

Fig. 3.1

One of Vacchiano's favorite recordings was Mahler's *Symphony No. 5* (fig. 3.2) with Bruno Walter conducting. This was the world première recording and Walter gave Vacchiano specific instruction on how to play the opening. "He had a unique way of subdividing the opening. It's in two, but in the music it says to not play in tempo. So he said to think of it in six (1-2-3-4-5-TTK T), so it makes it come out just right."[15]

Mahler, *Symphony No. 5*, Trumpet in B-flat
(original notation)

(Vacchiano's subdivision)

Fig. 3.2

Vacchiano was in such demand in New York City that he actually was contracted to record *Petrouchka* twice in one day: in the morning with Mitropoulos and the RCA Victor Symphony and in the afternoon with Stokowski and the Philharmonic.

> Stokowski, with his personality, took it very fast, while Mitropoulos wanted it very slow. That was one of the most difficult things I ever had to do! I was geared up to play it at a certain tempo and to play it so slow was torture! Now when I teach that solo, I tell all my students that story and that they have to be prepared to play it at different tempi, or else they'll be stuck!"[16]

When preparing for Bach's *Brandenburg Concerto No. 2*, or some other challenging Bach part that requires a high trumpet, the majority of trouble and discomfort comes from a shallow mouthpiece. Vacchiano instructed his students to practice those excerpts the same way he did, which was to practice fundamentals with the shallow mouthpiece on the B-flat trumpet. The sound will not be big and full, but it will allow the student to get used to the resistance and feel of the shallow mouthpiece. When playing the higher pitched trumpets, it is the mouthpiece that causes the greater difficulty rather than the instrument.[17]

Preparing for the Audition

When preparing a student for an audition, Vacchiano noted that it was important to be aware of the reason a trumpet position had become vacant. If the player was fired, you needed to know why. In most cases it was because the player had not performed to the highest professional standard. The following story is an example of just such a case.

> Very often in an audition the conductor asks a new player to play something that's been goofed by the guy they're replacing. I know a player who went to a major symphony orchestra and tried to play *Also Sprach Zarathustra* on B-flat trumpet. He missed the octave leap three concerts in a row and lost his job and his nerve because he used the wrong equipment. The first thing they are going to ask the new man is to play that excerpt. They want to find out if the man coming in could do what the other fellow couldn't. If he passes that first test, then they ask him other things.[18]

While Phil Smith was in his last semester of study with Vacchiano at Juilliard, Vacchiano drilled him weekly on every excerpt imaginable in preparation for the audition with the Chicago Symphony Orchestra. Smith gives the following recollection:

> I especially remember this story when I was preparing for the Chicago audition. Vacchiano would have me pull up Mahler's *Symphony No. 5* and he would say, "Alright Smith, I want you to play this. Now you see this note here, you will miss that and split this other one over here." It was like he wanted you to say, "I'll show you." After gaining my composure, I would play it and try not to have him psyche me out and miss anything. It was a game he used to develop psychological strength and mental toughness. This kind of training absolutely prepared me for my career as a principal trumpet player.[19]

Many orchestral auditions today require that you play the principal parts, even if the vacant seat is second or third. Vacchiano did not consider a true test for a second-chair player to be the *Brandenburg Concerto No. 2* or *Petrouchka*, but rather an excerpt like the low second trumpet duet from *Don Carlos* (fig. 3.3) by Verdi. Very few players can play this solo because it requires tremendous control of the low register. This was the excerpt that Toscanini auditioned Nat Prager on for second trumpet in the Philharmonic, and the figure is in Toscanini's own handwriting.[20] Vacchiano was interested in molding a complete musician, not just a principal trumpet player. He wanted his students to be prepared for the specific demands of each position.

Verdi, Don Carlos (in italics), Act IV, Part 2, Second Cornet in A

Fig. 3.3

CHAPTER FOUR

ACCHIANO'S RULES OF ORCHESTRAL PERFORMANCE

✦

A significant part of Vacchiano's pedagogy was teaching the student to play with the correct style. These rules were imparted to Vacchiano through his contact with many famous conductors and most importantly his teacher, Max Schlossberg. Vacchiano estimated the number of these rules to exceed two hundred. The rules found below, which I compiled and summarized as I worked with Mr. Vacchiano, are intended as a starting place for interpretation.

Articulation

The last note of a slur must match the articulation of the note that follows it. For example, if you have four sixteenth notes with the first two notes slurred and the third and fourth notes short, then the second note of the slur is short (fig. 4.1).

Fig. 4.1

In addition to the previous rule, the second two notes after the slur are not to be rushed.

All slurs are played with a feminine ending.[1]

When notes are slurred in pairs, as in the ascending and descending arpeggio in the "Ballerina's Dance" from *Petrouchka* (fig. 4.2), the second note is long if the first note is on the beat. If the slurred groupings start off the beat, the second note of the slur is short (even if not marked as a staccato).

Stravinsky, *Petrouchka*, "Ballerina's Dance," Trumpet in B-flat

Fig. 4.2

If two eighth notes are tied together and the first eighth note starts on a downbeat, the stress is on the beat (i.e. ONE-and TWO-and THREE-and, etc.). Those slurs must be long and played as smoothly as possible. If the eighth note gets turned around and the eighth note is on the "and" of beat two and then tied to the down beat, that is a short slur (fig. 4.3).

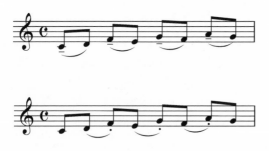

Fig. 4.3

"I have a question that's always asked: 'When the value of a note gets shorter (quarter, eighth, sixteenth, etc.), how is the length of each note treated?' I ask them in return, 'If you're going ten miles an hour and the note is one inch long, how long is the note if you are going twenty miles per hour?' They will all say a half-inch. This is wrong. If you're going twenty miles per hour it's twice as long. The faster you go the longer the notes will be, otherwise it will disappear. Consequently, when you double and triple tongue the double tongue has to be twice as long as the single tongue. The triple tongue is twice as long as the double tongue to counteract for the speed in the air.

"We always spread eighth-notes very short because the air could catch them very fast, but if you're playing at a terrific speed and you continue to play the eighth-notes short, they'll go by like a shot—you have to counteract it. In the old days we called this hammer tongue. They got the word from the piano. You put the pedal down in the piano and you hit the notes until you hear how they ring. They don't stop, that was called hammer tonguing."[2]

In a fast tempo: the quarter notes are long, eighth notes are short (played like a sixteenth note with a sixteenth rest) and the sixteenths are long, unless marked otherwise (fig. 4.4).

Fig. 4.4

When playing a fanfare in the middle of an orchestral piece, the shorter valued notes are the most important. The shorter notes need to be played louder than the longer notes. The short notes are what Vacchiano called the "money notes"—he was always concerned with what was going to be audible in the concert hall. It is the same concept with pickup notes—the pickup is always stronger in weight, which emphasizes the downbeat.

According to Doug Lindsay, "Vacchiano had a unique concept of how to play two eighth notes. He related it to how a timpanist plays two eighth notes with one stick. He said, 'When you play a single timpani with one stick, there has to be separation in those two eighth notes, because you hit it twice and lift. That is the way a trumpet player should play eighth notes.' He was not talking about a long lyric solo, but rather a Haydn symphony. This is a very useful concept in teaching the *Leonore* calls."[3]

Articulated scale-wise passages are usually legato, but when the intervals are larger than a third, they must be staccato.

One must use different approaches to different kinds of music. When playing Germanic music like Brahms, Wagner, and Bruckner, use a much softer and broader attack. But when playing an Italian opera, play shorter and lighter.

Rhythm

All eighth notes followed by or preceded by a sixteenth note automatically become a sixteenth note followed by a sixteenth rest.

If there is an eighth note that is slurred along with two sixteenth notes, then the sixteenths become thirty-seconds. A good example of this is the lyric solo at the end of Strauss's *Ein Heldenleben* (fig. 4.5).

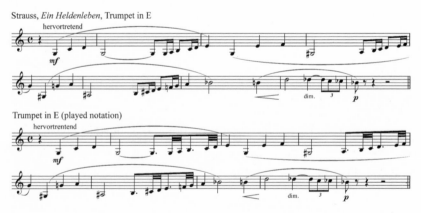

Fig 4.5

In playing fast sixteenth-note passages, feel the pulse in eighth notes. This gives steady rhythm and even technique.

With dotted eighths, the dot automatically becomes a rest.

Manny Laureano had this observation: "He addressed something that no one talks about anymore and that is the German sixteenths. The German dotted-eighth sixteenth figure is much heavier than the way we American precision oriented players try to do these days. Let's say you're playing a duet and on a given beat the first player has a triplet and the second has a dotted-eighth sixteenth. As American precisionists, we go out of our way to make sure that the sixteenth comes after the last note of the triplet. However, there was a time in musical history where the dotted figure and the 6/8 rhythm would sound much more similar.

"Everything had its context. In other words, for the opening of Schumann's *Symphony No. 2*, you played that sixteenth note slightly slower. But if you were playing Stravinsky, you would play a perfect, well-subdivided sixteenth. I had the exact same discussion on the same piece with Bud Herseth. These are the little tools that separate an experienced player from one who is green."[4]

There are several different types of sixteenth notes, for instance: German, French, and Italian. German is heavier—the Mahler sixteenth; the French is very light; and the Italian is kind of snappy.

In Italian music, sixteenth notes are short, in German they are long. Haydn and Mozart are short and light, like a clavichord. Bach is longer and legato, like an old organ.

In Mozart, the eighth-and-two-sixteenth rhythm is strict, but if the same rhythm is followed by a triplet, then the sixteenths become thirty-second notes.

"While explaining the dotted-eighth sixteenth eighth rhythm, Vacchiano said the word, 'Am-ster-dam.' He had a little song for *Ride of the Valkyries* and it matched up with subway stops. He recited all the subway stops from one place to another in that rhythm. So when he was playing the music, that's what was in his head. He said, 'You gotta kick this note; kick the little guy (i.e. the sixteenth) and then the last note is short—then wait to come in on time with the next one.' He was a *real* stickler on time," noted Robert Karon.[5]

The most important note rhythmically is the shortest valued note (i.e. a sixteenth note in a dotted-eighth sixteenth rhythm), because that is the hardest one with which to get the same amount of resonance and clarity when it is the mix of everything else. It must be played so it sounds exaggerated up close. If it is not played that way, the sixteenth is not heard out in the hall.

All dotted-eighth sixteenth notes are played as triplets (except when slurred) in German music. In Italian music they are played as thirty-second notes.

When there is a dotted-eighth sixteenth rhythm followed by a triplet, the sixteenth is treated as a thirty-second to emphasize the differentiation between the two rhythms. An example of this is found in the first trumpet part of "Goldenberg and Schmuyle" from Mussorgsky's *Pictures at an Exhibition* (fig. 4.6).

Mussorgsky, *Pictures at an Exhibition,* "Goldenberg and Schmuyle," Trumpet in C

Fig. 4.6

Phrasing

Manny Laureano said, "Vacchiano's lessons always focused on proper phrasing—very violinistic, string oriented phrasing. In fact, many of the markings I have in my excerpt books and solos were violin bowings. He hated when people accented the wrong beats—when they ended on a weak beat with an accent. He talked about so-called feminine ending. He made sure that when we had an arpeggio that rose upwards and ended on a weak beat, that we did a slight diminuendo away from the weak beat instead of the usual inclination that so many trumpet players have as they go higher where they power through and end up sounding like bad Italian tenors."[6]

"Vacchiano emphasized the idea of playing the architecture of a given measure properly. For instance, in the 'Promenade' from Mussorgsky's *Pictures at an Exhibition* [fig. 4.7] (which is in 5/4) a lot of people stress the F because it is the higher note, but it is the C that should be stressed. The D that follows should never be stressed, making sure that you are giving weight to the right notes of a measure, not just how it facilitates playing trumpet."[7]

Mussorgsky, *Pictures at an Exhibition*, "Promenade," Trumpet in C

Fig. 4.7

With regard to placing the proper pulse, you never accent the upbeat. An exception to this is in the "Ballerina's Dance" from Stravinsky's *Petrouchka* where there is an eighth and two sixteenths—you must emphasize the sixteenths, not the eighth notes.

Miscellaneous

Vacchiano had a great deal of useful advice for his students who had professional ambitions. It included:

The lower neighbor rule: this occurs where an accidental found earlier in the measure is cancelled later, even though a natural sign may be absent. When the accidental is on the lower neighbor (like a D, C-sharp, D) then later in that measure if there is another C that does not go back to the D, it becomes a C natural automatically.

One of the biggest things I do with my students is engraining cadences. We take all the cadences of all the exercises and we write them in every key. I have accumulated about 200. I have them on mimeograph to give to my students. This greatly increases their sight-reading abilities because their ears and mind are well versed in how each phrase ends.

Always play louder when below the staff. Vacchiano often used analogies to make these kinds of points easy to remember: "When you go into the basement, turn on the lights."

If you have a trill on a dotted note, you do not trill the dot. For instance, on a dotted quarter note, trill for one beat only.

Below low E, the trumpet is too rich to use vibrato. "It's like putting butter on butter."

Practice scale studies in Arban's as if they were an accompaniment to an aria.

Trill upper E to F-sharp using open and 2-3. Blow as if to play the E only.

For B to C-sharp trill, use 1-3 to 3.

Practice the following exercise (fig. 4.8) in all keys for Strauss's *Symphonia Domestica*.

Fig. 4.8

When a study ends as below (fig. 4.9), always stop on the C or corresponding note. That is the real end of the study. Stop, take a breath and then play the last two notes. They are like an "A-men."

Fig. 4.9

Never look at other players when they are playing.

If you are not the principal or section leader, do not offer suggestions unless you are asked.

Never practice someone else's part during a rehearsal.

CHAPTER FIVE

$\mathscr{P}$EDAGOGICAL METHODS

✦

Vacchiano's teaching career spanned seven decades as an instructor at The Juilliard School (1935–2002), Manhattan School of Music (1937–1999), Mannes College of Music (1937–1983), Queens College (1970–1973, 1991–1994), North Carolina School of the Arts (1973–1976), and Columbia Teachers College.[1] In addition to his tenure at these renowned music schools, he instructed many students at his home in Flushing, New York, from 1935 to 2005. Vacchiano estimated he privately taught over 2,000 students during his entire career.[2]

Vacchiano's professional teaching and playing careers began simultaneously when he joined the New York Philharmonic as third trumpet (and assistant principal) at the age of twenty-three. Due to the declining health of his former teacher, Max Schlossberg, Vacchiano was appointed to the faculty of The Juilliard School.

Teaching Style

The teaching style Vacchiano employed during his career was strikingly similar to the style learned during his studies with Max Schlossberg, focusing primarily on orchestral style, transposition, and the rudiments of playing the trumpet. Weekly lessons were comprised of studies from three main method books: Arban's *Complete Conservatory Method for Trumpet*, Saint-Jacome's *Grand Method for Trumpet or Cornet*, and

Sachse's *100 Studies for Trumpet*. In addition to these materials, Vacchiano frequently composed exercises specifically addressing the student's weaknesses. He eventually compiled these exercises into various étude books.[3]

The general approach in Vacchiano's teaching was very simple: build the strongest and most complete foundation possible to prepare the student for any and every situation. This foundation was developed by drilling the student on the basics of arpeggios, scales, transposition, articulation, and style. Malcolm McNab, a foremost Los Angeles studio musician, commented, "If you mastered everything he assigned you, you would be an incredible technician!"[4]

A typical first lesson with Vacchiano was very much the same for everyone. It did not matter if you were a professional or an amateur; he put every student through his paces to expose specific strengths and weaknesses. Initially, he checked the student's tone quality by having him or her play the simple exercises on page 40 (fig. 5.1) in the Arban method.

Arban, p. 40, #8

Fig. 5.1

After assessing the tone, he turned to page 73 to check the low register (G major scales) (fig. 5.2).

Arban, p. 73, #64

Fig. 5.2

Vacchiano then proceeded to check lip flexibility on page 44 (fig. 5.3).

Fig. 5.3

Beginning on page 155 (fig. 5.4), the student's triple and double tonguing were tested.

Fig. 5.4

The chord studies on pages 142–151 (fig. 5.5) determined the understanding of chord structure and harmony.

Fig. 5.5

Scales and various articulation patterns were examined both in the Arban and Saint-Jacome methods. The interval studies beginning on page 125 of the Arban (fig. 5.6) were used for ear training and flexibility.[5]

Fig. 5.6

In addition to playing these exercises at the suggested tempi, Vacchiano advised that in order to develop the proper orchestral weight and heaviness of tone, these pages be practiced at an extremely slow speed with each note maintaining a consistent timbre in all registers. Finally, the lesson was rounded-out with sight-reading and transposition work from various étude books.

Each student had a unique introduction into Vacchiano's pedagogy and personality, oftentimes mixed with both humor and seriousness. Al Ligotti, professor emeritus of trumpet at the University of Georgia, recalls how poignant Vacchiano could be while making a specific point:

> For my first lesson I had prepared two études the best I could, one from Arban and one from Saint-Jacome. After playing about the first three-quarters of the Arban étude, he stopped me. I will never forget what happened next: he reached into his pocket and took out a nickel (in those days, it only cost a nickel to ride the subway). He flipped it into the air and it landed on the music stand. He said, "You see that nickel? With that nickel and the way you play, you could ride the subway! You're playing all these little notes and they don't mean anything. Play a C major scale in quarter-notes in one octave from low C to middle C at MM=72." I played them and he responded, "You played eight notes up and eight notes down. What did you accomplish? Every note leads to another note, then to a third note and suddenly you're playing *music*. There is music in everything you do. Any time the mouthpiece goes to your lips, you *must* play music." From that point on, it was like somebody turned on the lights to the world.[6]

Lee Soper, a New York freelance artist, chuckled when he remembered his first lesson:

> The first time I met Bill, my knees were shaking. I was straight out of the West Point Band and very happy to be a civilian again. I walked in wearing multi-colored bell-bottom pants with vertical stripes. He looked at me and said, "Hey Soper, did

you forget to take your pajama bottoms off?" That was my first lesson. It was that kind of humor that broke the ice and made you feel calm and relaxed.[7]

The overall concept of sound and weight was of paramount importance to Vacchiano. He would practice long tones for hours just to get the perfect sound. He said, "Many students come to me not understanding the significance of the weight of the sound. The trumpet must come through with a clear tone in a 100-piece orchestra. Tone is everything; technique is secondary."[8]

Mario Guarneri, formerly with the Los Angeles Philharmonic, tells how Vacchiano taught the concept of weight and sound in his lessons:

> I was working hard trying to make everything sound perfect on the opening of *Don Juan*. Bill was standing by an open window looking down to the street while I was playing. When I finished what I thought was a pretty good performance, he said, "Guarneri, that was terrible," but with a warm smile on his face. I wasn't surprised by that response since that was his usual evaluation of almost everything I did in my lessons. What he said next has stayed with me through my career and is really basic to my music making and teaching. He said, "I was looking down on the street while you were playing and not one person stopped and looked up." That was very instructional and inspiring.[9]

The weekly lesson consisted of studies from various method books or orchestral excerpts. The entirety of each lesson was comprised of simultaneous sight-reading and transposition. A typical lesson took the following course: two or three études in Sachse (all in the hardest transposition possible), a few pages in both Arban and Saint-Jacome to work on fundamentals and technique, a wide variety of études, and a few orchestral excerpts (always in at least three different transpositions). None of these exercises, études, or excerpts was ever played in the written key. Upon completing the sight-reading of an étude, Vacchiano would say, "Okay, work that up." Over the course of the following week the student zealously "worked up" each étude that was sight-read in the lesson. Vacchiano, however, rarely requested to hear an étude from the previous week. He did this to cover as much material as possible with each student. He was more interested in how well the student could play without preparation, instead of what could be accomplished after hours of practice. It was the musical concepts that mattered the most.

Many of Vacchiano's students noted the fact that they never played more than a few consecutive measures during a lesson because of the intense sight-reading and transposition requirements. Vacchiano incessantly stopped them to demand correct transposition, rhythm, and style. Consequently, Vacchiano very rarely heard the polished and rehearsed capabilities of his students. Gerard Schwarz, Music Director of the Seattle Symphony, reminisced about Vacchiano's response after hearing his student recital at Juilliard:

> I remember when I was studying with Bill at Juilliard I still felt (after having studied with him already for three years) that he had never really heard me play. So I arranged a recital and I asked him if he would come. He said he couldn't because he was too busy and he didn't like to go to recitals. I said I would arrange the recital around his schedule. I had to remind him of his promise to attend on several different occasions. Finally, it was the night of the recital and the Philharmonic had a matinee, so he was available. Of course, when I saw him there I was shocked and thrilled at the same time! I played my recital and when the concert was over Vacchiano came backstage and he said to me, "That was terrific! I had no idea you could play like that!"[10]

Even though the lessons were based on sight-reading, Vacchiano had a methodical and strategic plan for each student. Mario Guarneri comments on his weekly lesson routine:

> If Vacchiano gave you page 142 in Arban (major triads), then all week you would practice viciously on them. The next week you would come in ready to play them from memory and then

he would say, "Let's read the minors." So you would fall all over them and he would say, "You don't know these very well, you had better learn them. What have you been practicing all week?" So you would work even harder on those and then the next week we went on to the seventh chords. It was always continuous. My two years at Juilliard were certainly the most intense period of practicing that I ever had in my life.[11]

Malcolm McNab describes the atmosphere created by Vacchiano during his weekly lessons:

While you were turning to a certain page in Arban, Saint-Ja-come, or Sachse, he would be solfèging the étude in the key you were about to play, as well as the desired tempo. He was already putting pressure on you before you had even found the right page. Then he would say, "Okay, you ready? D trumpet and change articulation: slur two, tongue two." You had to concentrate on an extremely high level. He would put you on the spot and then you'd fall on your butt. The idea was that you would be so embarrassed that you'd go home and practice so it would not happen again.[12]

The purpose of this type of instruction was not to be intimidating, but rather to create a professional environment for the student, allowing him or her to perform under pressure in the professional world. Thomas Stevens, retired principal trumpet of the Los Angeles Philharmonic, attributes his success in overcoming these types of pressures to his studies with Vacchiano:

After enduring the rigors of Vacchiano lessons, situations like studio recordings or concerts with no rehearsals were never problematic for me. I have always believed this was why he taught in the manner he did, one which simulated the actual pressures and requirements of the professional music business. Moreover, he always concentrated on what I could *not* do. If I were to come in and play something very well, he would stop me and move on to something else. He once remarked he didn't want to hear a recital; he was there to help me with my liabilities rather than my assets.[13]

Vacchiano possessed a very specific ability to critique a student's playing and immediately identify the weaknesses. He understood how each weakness, no matter how small, could evolve into a fatal flaw that inhibited the student's progress. He enjoyed the challenge of each personality regardless of how headstrong the student was and he would not move on until the problem was fixed. Ron Anderson, former principal trumpet of the New York City Ballet, expressed his appreciation for Vacchiano's relentless critique: "The cleanliness he hounded out of me during my lessons allowed me to play both accurately and passionately. Had he not ironed out my weakness, I would not have been able to do all the things I have done."[14]

Transposition

One of the first things that come to mind when former students reminisce about their lessons with Vacchiano is the synonymity of the two words "Vacchiano" and "transposition." Certainly, this started with those early solfège lessons with Mr. DiNobile.

Of the many types of exercises for technique and facility on the trumpet, the best exercise for ear training is transposition. The purpose of transposition is to address the student's overall musicianship by developing the mind and ear. A note is usually cracked when the student does not hear the note prior to it being sounded. If the player attempts to play a G-sharp, an F-sharp or an A-sharp may come out instead. Consistent practice of transposition will greatly reduce the chances of cracking or splitting notes because it trains the ears to be more active in the process of reading music.[15]

Doug Lindsay remembers Vacchiano telling him how he would practice transposition on the subway.

> Vacchiano would say, "When I was in school going to Juilliard, I cut off the valve section of a trumpet and I made a leather

holster for it. I would carry it with me on the subway, pull it out and transpose my étude books." A lot of his best work was done on the subway![16]

Vacchiano said on many occasions, "Nothing will develop a musician better than transposition. Those players who cannot transpose are merely buglers; those who can are musicians. If you can play the Sachse book in every key, you can play anywhere."

Vacchiano liked to relate this story about Miles Davis's sense of humor:

> When Miles Davis was taking lessons from me at Juilliard he had never had to study transposition before. In the first lessons I was trying to teach the basic methodology and said, "You've got a B-flat trumpet, the music has three flats, and the part says 'Trumpet in E.' Where does that put your trumpet [What key are you playing in now]?" Davis looked at me confidently and said, "As far as I'm concerned, right back in the case!"[17]

Manny Laureano recalled his studies with Vacchiano on transposition: "The study of transposition was another constant; and God bless him, he always had us do them on the B-flat trumpet. You pulled out your Sachse book and the B-flat at the same time."[18] During one of Jeffrey Silberschlag's lessons, Vacchiano told him, "When you stop practicing the Sachse book, you have stopped practicing!"[19]

In his teaching, Vacchiano taught three main ways of transposition: clefs, intervals, and numbers. He tended to favor clefs in lessons and his own playing, but he did not require students to use this method exclusively; he merely wanted them to understand the various ways to transpose.

While teaching orchestral excerpts in lessons, Vacchiano insisted that each passage be played in at least three different keys and on three different trumpets. The purpose and end result enabled the student to play whichever trumpet made the concert or recording session easiest. His contention was if you walked into any gig with a B-flat, D, and piccolo trumpet (with both A and B-flat slides), you would be prepared to play anything in any transposition. Laureano recalled the importance of Vacchiano's relentless study of transposition:

> During my first concert as principal trumpet with the Seattle Symphony, we had to play two very heavy programs back-to-back at an outdoor season opener. Of course, the last piece we played was the final movement of Tchaikovsky's *Symphony No. 4*. The first time through was fine, but by the second time I was thinking, "I'm starting to feel a little heat!" So I reached down and picked up my D trumpet and read the entire last movement in that transposition, even though I had never played it before on the D trumpet. All of these transpositions were fresh in my mind and it was exactly what Vacchiano had trained me for.[20]

Tone Production

According to Vacchiano, the most important aspect of an orchestral trumpet player is his tone. "To the true artist, the sound is primary; technique is secondary. I used to play two hours a day of just long notes and slurs to get a beautiful sound. In an audition, they don't judge you on technique, it is what you sound like. It's the *sound*."[21]

Vacchiano stated that by the time he came to New York in 1931 to study at the Institute of Musical Art, he basically had finished developing his technique.[22] It was at this point that he decided to focus on transposition and tone production. His favorite exercise for developing an even tone in all registers was found on page 125 of the Arban method. He would hold each note of the line for one beat at a very slow tempo, focusing on the weight of the sound.

Former student and longtime colleague, Carmine Fornarotto, made the following observations during his years of study with Vacchiano:

> Bill was a listener and occasionally a demonstrator. Bill knew that most of us listened to the broadcasts of the Philharmonic and he expected us to grow and follow his lead. Bill didn't have a dominant personality. He was a very mellow, laid-back hu-

man being. He wanted you to grow into your own musical self. He knew the music and he knew you knew the music, but he wanted to know if you knew it stylistically. "Go listen to some records. Go spend hours and hours a week listening to Boston, Cleveland, and NBC. Go listen to all the other first trumpet players. Go listen to them and see how you want to play in relationship to them; and of course come listen to me."[23]

The prelude to Wagner's *Parsifal* is a perfect excerpt to help develop not only proper orchestral tone, but also advanced breath control. Vacchiano had his students practice this by transposing it to the lowest possible key. After playing it a couple of times in that transposition, he had them transpose up a half step. This continued until the student reached the original key and higher. After playing the excerpt at a lower transposition with very little resistance, breath control was no longer an issue and the tone and timbre would be uniform because the student would know all the pitch tendencies in every key. This practice routine also encouraged proper development of range and endurance.[24]

Stephen Chenette tells the following story to demonstrate the effectiveness of this approach:

> At one point in my studies with Vacchiano, I got a quiver in my sound and I still don't know why. Instead of trying to figure it out physically, Vacchiano said, "Practice two things: the Sachse study #30 (which is a beautiful study) and the melody to Wagner's *Rienzi* and play them in all the keys, even down to low F-sharp—that will fix it." I did those things and they fixed it.[25]

Intonation

Intonation on the trumpet can be very challenging, especially for the younger player. Just as the orchestral sound was integral to Vacchiano's teaching, so was consistent intonation on all the various pitched trumpets. In an effort to sensitize the student's ear to the pitch tendencies of the instrument, Vacchiano demanded false fingerings to be played for several months. Practicing in this manner for an extended period of time resulted in the student hearing the intonation with the alternate fingerings to the opposite extreme. When Vacchiano gave permission to play with regular fingerings, the student adjusted the pitch instinctively rather than by guessing.

Another intonation technique Vacchiano used consisted of the student pulling out the tuning slide to play flat. In the following lesson, Vacchiano had the student push the tuning slide all the way in and play sharp. He did not want the student to get accustomed to playing in one spot. At times, the piano, orchestra, or band may be flat or sharp to what is normal. If the student has occasionally practiced in this manner, such instances will not be problematic because it will not be a foreign feeling. For extreme situations, Vacchiano carried an extension to place between the mouthpiece and leadpipe to elongate the instrument. "I always carry an extension in my pocket if I ever have to play in church or a theatre. It practically puts the trumpet in another key, facilitating the intonation challenges."[26]

Tonguing

Vacchiano spent a significant amount of time on shaping the student's attack and cleaning up articulation:

> Over my last forty-five years of teaching experience I have noticed that some students play with a lighter attack and other students have a tendency to play with a heavier attack. We can compensate for this difference in the mouthpiece. A bigger hole and open throat will slow the student with a lighter attack down. A snugger hole and throat will speed up the student with the heavier attack. Even though this may speed up his tongue, many times that same player needs a rounded rim to soften his attack.[27]

In the preface to *The Art of Double Tonguing* and *The Art of Triple Tonguing*, Vacchiano expresses the importance of multiple tonguing:

The ability to triple and double tongue is a great asset in perfecting technique and an indispensable prerequisite to any trumpeter embarking on a performance or teaching career. I have found that the attention devoted to the study and acquisition of these skills is rarely in proportion to their performance. It is my hope that my two books, *The Art of Double Tonguing* and *The Art of Triple Tonguing*, will help remedy this deficiency.[28]

In his thirty-eight years with the Philharmonic, Vacchiano spent a considerable amount of time playing compositions with intricate articulation patterns by composers like Stravinsky, Ravel, and Rimsky-Korsakov. Vacchiano's use of multiple articulations, while sometimes unorthodox, was very effective in his own playing while the same methods challenged his students to correct their deficiencies. Many students commented during interviews that Vacchiano taught them a certain articulation pattern that they did not use for several years until one day when they realized how that pattern could facilitate a certain passage. These were the tools Vacchiano gave his students that enabled them to perform any type of composition. Even though a specific articulation might be used only a handful of times, it was still a critical component of the complete musician Vacchiano molded.[29]

Two examples that illustrate this are Shostakovich's *Concerto for Piano, Trumpet, and Strings* (fig. 5.7) and Rimsky-Korsakov's *Capriccio Espagnol* (fig. 5.8). The end of Shostakovich's concerto contains a rather tricky passage that at first glance appears to be a simple double-tongue pattern. Vacchiano, however, wanted to be able to play this faster if the conductor desired while maintaining clarity of sound and articulation. He came to the conclusion of using a triple-tongue pattern over the duple grouping:

Shostakovich, *Concerto for Piano, Trumpet (in B-flat), and Strings*, Mvt. 3

Fig. 5.7

This second example by Rimsky-Korsakov (fig. 5.8) does not change the grouping or pattern, but rather the desired aural result. Burton Sachs tells how Vacchiano solved this problem for him:

> There are two places in the first and second trumpet parts of the third movement of Rimsky-Korsakov's *Capriccio Espagnol*—measure ten and four measures before letter K—where my conductor could not hear the sixteenth-note triplet I played. I was playing it, but nothing I did brought this out to the conductor's satisfaction. I took the problem to Bill at my next lesson. He told me to triple tongue my part and have the second player slur the triplets with me. At the next rehearsal the conductor said, "Perfect! Now I hear the part." From that day in 1957, I have always told the second player to slur there. That problem has never occurred again.[30]

Rimsky-Korsakov, *Capriccio Espagnol*, Mvt. III - Alborada, Trumpet 1 & 2 in B-flat
(original notation played by Trumpet 1 only)

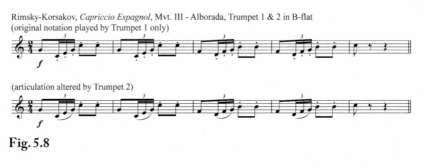

(articulation altered by Trumpet 2)

Fig. 5.8

No matter how unorthodox these ideas seemed on the surface, Vacchiano still experimented in order to achieve the best aural result. Passing these processes and results to his students gave them the tools to succeed as both a performer and problem-solver.

William Vacchiano in high school, ca. 1928. Collection of Jo Ann Vacchiano.

Rafaello Vacchiano, ca. age 40. Collection of Jo Ann Vacchiano.

Max Schlossberg, trumpeter with the New York Philharmonic and Vacchiano's teacher at The Juilliard School. Collection of Jo Ann Vacchiano.

Ethel Josephine LaParde, Vacchiano's future wife, in her mid-twenties. Collection of Jo Ann Vacchiano.

This sketch of William Vacchiano by artist Edward Barnard Lintott appeared in *The Philharmonic-Symphony Orchestra of New York* (1939), which featured drawings of many of the Philharmonic's members. "The Philharmonic-Symphony Orchestra of New York. Season of 1939–1940" by William G. King, illustrations by Edward Barnard Lintott (New York: Philharmonic-Symphony League of New York, 1939).

A young William Vacchiano, ca. 1940. Collection of Lee Soper.

It was Georges Mager who first told Vacchiano that with such a long face, he needed a deeper mouthpiece. This was a revelation to Vacchiano, and he used this concept to become a master at matching a student to the proper mouthpiece based on facial structure. Collection of Lee Soper.

Vacchiano always spent two weeks each summer at his in-laws' tobacco farm in Nathalie, Virginia. Collection of Jo Ann Vacchiano.

Vacchiano was well known for his subtle sense of humor, as evidenced in this introspective pose, while "fingering" the trumpet upside down. Courtesy the New York Philharmonic Archives.

Presentation to Mayor Fiorello LaGuardia of the newly released recording of Debussy's *Rhapsody for Clarinet and Orchestra*, 1941 (l–r) Benny Goodman, Sir John Barbirolli, LaGuardia, Harry Glantz (trumpet), Vacchiano (trumpet), Mario Falcone (trombone), Nat Prager (trumpet), Vincenzo Vani (tuba), Bruno Labate (oboe). Courtesy of the New York Philharmonic Archives.

Vacchiano poses with youngsters as part of the New York Philharmonic Red Cross Drive during World War II. Courtesy of the New York Philharmonic Archives.

Meeting of principal players with conductor Bruno Walter in spring 1947, preceding the beginning of Walter's first season as Musical Advisor of the New York Philharmonic. Courtesy of the New York Philharmonic Archives.

New York Philharmonic trumpet section in rehearsal, 1950 (l–r), James Smith, Vacchiano, Nat Prager, Johnny Ware. Courtesy of the New York Philharmonic Archives.

In rehearsal with the New York Philharmonic, 1958. Photo by Nix Rybakov. Courtesy of the New York Philharmonic Archives.

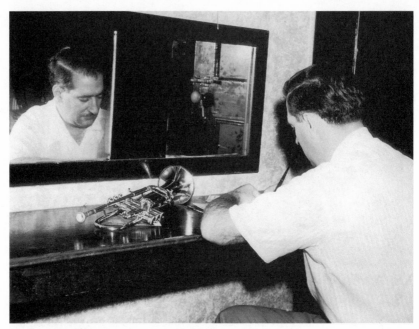

Signing checks during an orchestra break. Collection of Phyllis Stork.

New York Philharmonic brass players, ca. 1958 (l–r) James Chambers, Joseph Singer, Ed Herman, Vacchiano, Bill Bell. Courtesy of the New York Philharmonic Archives.

Vacchiano holds the F trumpet on which he recorded Bach's *Brandenburg Concerto No. 2* and *Mass in B Minor*. Collection of Jo Ann Vacchiano.

William Vacchiano with just a few of his "tools of the trade" collection in the early 1960s. Collection of Lee Soper.

Vacchiano demonstrating excerpts to Atsuyoshi Takayama during a trumpet lesson in a Tokyo Hotel, May 9, 1961. ©1961 Atsuyoshi Takayama.

Johnny Ware, Ed Herman, and Vacchiano outside the Lincoln Center for the Performing Arts Executive Offices, ca. 1970. Collection of Jo Ann Vacchiano.

Vacchiano was a Life Member of the New York Brass Conference for Scholarships and is seen here with Maynard Ferguson and the NYBCS founder Dr. Charles Colin, late 1970s. Collection of Jo Ann Vacchiano.

At a later NYBCS, Vacchiano talks with his former student, Wynton Marsalis. Collection of Sam Goldfarb.

Vacchiano presenting a master class in the 1970s. Collection of Jo Ann Vacchiano.

Vacchiano came up from the audience to perform Leroy Anderson's *Bugler's Holiday* with Canadian Brass trumpeters (and former students) Fred Mills and Ronald Romm, early 1980s. Other members: Graeme Page (horn), Eugene Watts (trombone), Charles Daellenbach (tuba). Collection of Philip Varriale.

Vacchiano poses backstage at Avery Fisher Hall in Lincoln Center, New York, after a guest performance by the Los Angeles Philharmonic, ca. 1986. (l–r) Vacchiano, Thomas Stevens, Irving Bush, Don Green. Collection of Thomas Stevens.

Frank Kaderabek, Vacchiano, Armando Ghitalla, and a supporter of the Streitwieser Trumpet Museum in Pottstown, Pennsylvania on September 15, 1991. Collection of Jo Ann Vacchiano.

Vacchiano and former student Lee Soper, on the occasion of Bill's 80ᵗʰ birthday—May 23, 1992. Collection of Lee Soper.

Vacchiano's 85ᵗʰ birthday party at The Juilliard School, seen here with Chris Gekker, Mark Gould, Ray Mase, and Phil Smith, May 1997. ©2002 Peter Schaaf.

Old friends Vacchiano and Johnny Ware at Vacchiano's 85th birthday party at the Juilliard School, May 1997. ©2002 Peter Schaaf.

Vacchiano's right-hand fix-it man—John "Peppy" Pettinato. Collection of Jo Ann Vacchiano.

William Vacchiano always dressed impeccably, seen here in the late 1990s with his "trademark pencil" close at hand. Collection of Jo Ann Vacchiano.

Vacchiano out for a walk in 2001. Collection of Lee Soper.

Vacchiano said his greatest honor was receiving the Honorary Doctorate from The Juilliard School on May 23, 2002—his 91st birthday. Seated (l–r) Vacchiano, Julius Baker, Alfredo Corvino; standing (l–r) Renée Fleming, Ellis Marsalis, Jr., Marian Seldes. ©2002 Peter Schaaf.

Vacchiano always composed at the bench of his living room baby grand piano. Collection of Jim Shugert.

The studio in Vacchiano's basement was both immaculate and eclectic, with mugs, reference books, photographs, the fan that whirred incessantly in lessons on warm days, and even a ship's wheel. Collection of Lee Soper.

$\mathcal{V}$ACCHIANO'S USE OF EQUIPMENT

The Mouthpiece

As each Vacchiano student attests, Vacchiano possessed an uncanny knowledge of the inner workings of the mouthpiece and how to find the right mouthpiece for each student. He stated:

> If you have a problem with your feet, you change your shoes. If you have a problem with your eyes, you get different glasses. Why should the lips be different? If someone is playing on the wrong mouthpiece he will never know the difference. If you give a student a mouthpiece that doesn't fit him, you may hinder his career.[1]

This knowledge came from many years of personal experience, as well as analyzing each student's embouchure and facial structure. The first time Vacchiano became aware of the importance of the mouthpiece is related in the following story:

> One day, I was walking on 57th Street and I met Georges Mager. I was pretty depressed about my playing. After I told him what mouthpiece I had, he explained that it was too small for me and then proceeded to give me a copy of his mouthpiece. That night we were doing *Don Juan* and I kept kicking my second trumpet

player and telling him, "Don't double; don't double!" I thought
he was doubling me because my playing was so loud![2]

He continued:

> I went from this crazy, small mouthpiece I'd been using to the
> one that he was using. It doubled my sound, my range, my
> speed of tonguing. Everything just opened right up. I have a
> large face and here I was using that tiny mouthpiece! I didn't
> even know it until I met him and I saw what was possible. If I
> hadn't met him, I probably would never have known that these
> things were possible until, perhaps, much later in my life. This
> was 1933 or 1934, before I joined the orchestra. I used it for
> about a year, and then I realized that it was even too big for me,
> so I went to [George] Bukur. This was another lucky thing for
> me because he had a special backbore that was given to him by a
> Mr. Schmidt in Germany. He made the mouthpiece just a little
> bit smaller and, with the new backbore, it really did the trick. It
> gave me just the kind of sound I was looking for.[3]

Another example Vacchiano gives of the importance of mouthpiece
selection involves Bruno Jaenicke, former principal horn of the Philharmonic:

> This is a true story of a really great horn player, Bruno Jaenicke,
> who was principal horn in the Philharmonic. At the begin-
> ning of one of our seasons, Jaenicke seemed to be having a little
> trouble. We all looked the other way and were apprehensive.
> A few weeks later, as if a cloud had been lifted, Mr. Jaenicke
> sounded great again. When we asked him the reason, he said
> he tried to change his mouthpiece. He was in his sixties and
> should not have tried to improve such fine playing. Although
> the above story may seem like a contradiction of my theories,
> don't be afraid to experiment with new mouthpieces. Mr. Jae-
> nicke's case was different; here was a great player who could've
> been destroyed by a bad mouthpiece. Of course he knew good
> from bad, so no damage was done.[4]

Most trumpet manufacturers include a relatively small mouthpiece with each new trumpet. Vacchiano hypothesized that this enabled many young players to play with a good range quickly. He estimated that one out of every ten students continued to play after a year or two, so it does not matter to the other eight or nine what they play. The one or two students who have the talent and desire to continue studying have been dealt a great disservice due to the mouthpiece, because the lips will outgrow the mouthpiece. If the manufacturer included a large mouthpiece, this could discourage the student early on and dissuade him from playing the trumpet. Careful guidance by the teacher is needed to assist the student in finding the right mouthpiece at the right time. "An aspiring pianist does not have this headache. All keyboards are the same!"[5] "The mouthpiece is ninety-nine percent of the battle. You can't change your lips to fit the mouthpiece, but you can change the mouthpiece to fit the lips."[6]

Vacchiano spent countless hours each week with Vincent Bach and John "Peppy" Pettinato where they studied all aspects of the mouthpiece by combining every possible variable.[7] Vacchiano estimated that he had accumulated about 500 mouthpieces during his teaching career. This type of curiosity and experimentation, coupled with privately teaching over 2,000 students, made Vacchiano an authority on mouthpieces.

Diagram of the Mouthpiece

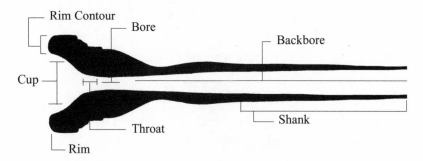

Fig. 6.1

Rim Diameter

The rim diameter of a mouthpiece is the uppermost portion that directly comes in contact with the lips. In order to find the right mouthpiece for each student, the first element Vacchiano considered was the correct rim diameter. The length of the upper lip directly determines the appropriate rim diameter for each student. If the upper lip is long, then a wider diameter is more suitable. If the upper lip is very thin and short, then a smaller diameter is advised. The common misconception is that a large rim diameter gives you more sound. Vacchiano's contention was that the cup depth affects the tone more than the diameter: "You cannot get as much sand in a one pound bag as you can in a two pound bag—the same is true with the mouthpiece. If you want more sand (i.e. tone and volume), you must increase the size of the bag (i.e. cup) rather than the mouth of the bag (i.e. rim diameter).[8]

Rim Shape and Contour

After the appropriate rim diameter is determined, the next aspect of the mouthpiece to consider is the shape and contour of the rim. When selecting a suitable rim for the student, the most important thing to consider is comfort. It is essential to find a rim that is comfortable and then match it with other components of the mouthpiece. "You can use dozens of different cups with impunity if you keep the same rim. In spite of the stories of how many times I changed mouthpieces, I always kept the same rim. I was not out to be a hero."[9]

Al Ligotti, who played extra with the Philharmonic for eleven years, confirmed Vacchiano's claim:

> For the Friday and Sunday afternoon concerts, Bill wore a vest that had three pockets on each side. I would watch him as he stocked each pocket with a different mouthpiece so he could easily switch mouthpieces during the concert. He could swap mouthpieces in the middle of a solo and you would never know.

He always had one mouthpiece as home base, all the others he switched to were very similar; there were no major changes that would throw his embouchure off.[10]

The rim of the mouthpiece has many variables. The following terms are used to describe these facets: high point, low point, round, flat, full cushion, semi-cushion, thin, thick, bite, and "under-bite" (or "under-belly").[11]

Vacchiano believed that a student with thick or fleshy lips (i.e. red/supple part of lips showing with the mouthpiece in place), would most likely use a very thin rim; and, vice-versa, a student with thin lips would likely use a thick rim. The student with thicker lips does not need as much support from the rim as the player with thinner lips. "I used the thinnest rim of all the trumpet players I have ever met. I used the same width rim that a French horn player uses. It can cut down on your endurance, but I had plenty of endurance because I developed it."[12]

The next aspect to consider is the high point of the rim (fig. 6.2). A rim that has a high point (on the outside, inside, or middle) gives the player a lighter sound. A flat rim (with no high point) does just the opposite by facilitating a fuller sound because it connects with, and uses more of, the lip's surface.

High point of the rim

Fig. 6.2

The bite, or inside edge of the rim, has a tremendous effect on flexibility, attack, and endurance. Vacchiano's theory was that a rounded bite will allow slurring and advanced flexibilities to be less labored while a sharp bite will exaggerate the percussiveness of the attack. A student who wishes to soften his attack will prefer a rounded bite; vice-versa, the student who desires a sharper attack might gravitate to a sharper bite. "The inner edge of my mouthpiece is so round that it will never cut. I tell my pupils that there is a big difference between a butter knife and a razor blade."[13]

Lacking the modern technology of today, Vacchiano often altered a student's mouthpiece right on the spot with rather crude tools. "Sometimes he took your mouthpiece and carved it right there. He would get a potato peeler out and take off part of the rim. Mostly, he would reshape rims—he would carve off the outside rim because it was a little high."[14]

In the context of mouthpiece rims, Vacchiano explained why the attack is critical in an orchestra:

> During auditions, the most important thing the committee listens to is the attack. For example, in the Brahms symphonies, many times the trumpet must come in without any type of percussive attack—the sound must just appear. This type of attack can be corrected by using a rounded rim with a rounded bite. The rim must not be rounded too much, because it will take away some of the punch that is needed for louder, more aggressive playing.[15]

In many cases, a decrease in endurance is caused by the loss of proper blood circulation to the lips. If a student is using a rim that is too thin, it may cut off or reduce circulation in the lips, thus endurance becomes an issue. In an effort to increase circulation and obtain more endurance, many lab band players use a full cushion rim (fig. 6.3).[16] A full cushion rim is an exaggerated version of a wide rim. This rim works on the same principle as a snowshoe. The width, or area, of the snowshoe keeps you from falling into the snow. The cushion rim distributes pressure over a wider surface area, allowing blood to the lips and reducing the possibilities of fatigue, swelling, and stiffness. A semi-cushion rim is advised for most orchestral players. This rim offers increased endurance while maintaining the flexibility and attack a full cushion rim may hinder.[17]

Cushion Rim

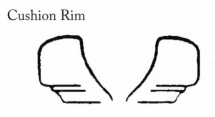

Fig. 6.3

If the student feels like his or her lips are touching the bottom of the cup, it means more room is needed in the underbelly. In order to create more room for the lips, the underbelly must be slightly carved inward without making the cup deeper. The lips will move more freely and high range will not be sacrificed.[18]

The Cup

The cup is the most important factor of the mouthpiece because it determines the overall sound. It also has a profound effect on range and intonation. As long as a comfortable rim has been established, the student can change the depth and shape of the cup for various styles of music without harming the embouchure.

Again, the first thing to consider is the fleshiness of the lips. If the lips are fleshy and protrude into the mouthpiece, the mouthpiece, in effect, becomes shallower. In this case, a deeper cup is advised to compensate for the displacement of the total volume of the cup. The opposite is true for the player whose lips are thin and do not protrude into the cup. It is possible for this player to use a slightly shallower mouthpiece than that of the fleshy-lipped player to attain a similar timbre. Vacchiano often used the following analogy referring to cup depth: "A tall person wears short heels and a short person wears tall heels," meaning that if the student has thick, fleshy lips they will most likely need a thinner rim with a larger cup and vice-versa.[19]

A cup that is too shallow may result in split or cracked attacks, especially in the upper register. In addition to using a more-rounded rim bite for delicate attacks, a deeper, more "V-shaped" cup can also provide a similar result. "James Burke told me years ago that his days of cracking were over when he went from a Bach 'C' cup (fig. 6.4) to a 'B' cup (fig. 6.5). The second movement of Brahms's *Symphony No. 2* is very soft and extremely difficult. I used to use a very deep cup for these few bars and relax."[20]

"C" Cup

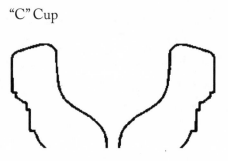

Fig. 6.4

"V-Shaped" Cup

Fig. 6.5

The cup depth can also affect articulation in the low register. A shallower cup offers more resistance and control of intonation in the low register, while a deeper cup has less resistance and a tendency to go flat in pitch. The general principle Vacchiano followed was this: Low notes have less resistance than high notes and a shallow cup has more resistance than a deep cup. If a deep cup (with not much resistance) is used to play a low passage (also with very little resistance), then the result will be one of tubbiness and troublesome intonation. The opposite is also true; if a cup that is too shallow (with significant resistance) is used to play in the high register (also with much resistance), then the tone will be pinched and the pitch will go sharp. "When I played something in the low register, I usually resorted to a shallower mouthpiece to gain greater control over those notes."[21]

The timbre and color of sound are directly related to cup depth. A shallow cup has a brighter, more brilliant sound than a deeper cup. A former student, Louis Ranger, relates the following story of how Vacchiano used a wide variety of mouthpieces to develop the student's sound concept:

> Vacchiano used mouthpieces in a therapeutic manner. If he decided the attack was too heavy, he would say, "Okay, play this 7D for a week" with the idea that the attack would be magnified so one would have to attack lighter. If he wanted the student to play brighter he'd say, "You had better play this 1A for a week." So it was necessary to work like mad to get any kind of brightness at all.[22]

Scott Whitener, professor of music at Rutgers University, recalled this about Vacchiano's association of mouthpieces and sound.

> At the time that I studied with him, he played frequently in lessons. He did not usually play on his regular mouthpiece, however, and he seemed to be experimenting. He had a little case with four or five mouthpieces on the table beside his chair, and he would select one and play a passage or étude on it. He didn't seem to be giving a demonstration, only experimenting with the mouthpiece. Only once or twice did he show me his regular mouthpieces. One of these was Mager's mouthpiece. I wasn't

very enthused with changing mouthpieces and was resisting his advice at one lesson. I told him that I wanted to stay with the one I was using because I liked the sound. He took Mager's mouthpiece out of the little case and asked me to play on it. It is very large (17.8 mm diameter). I had an unbelievable sound but then discovered I couldn't get above the G above the staff. He then looked at me and said with great emotion, "Mager's mouthpiece is the only one that I have ever been happy with my sound on, but it is too large. I can't play it."[23]

Two basic types of jaw deformities can cause difficulties in playing the trumpet. The player with a protruding jaw finds it best to use a shallower cup because his upper lip is usually not in the cup as much as the player with a receding jaw, who puts more upper lip into the mouthpiece. If the deformity is not severe, a simple change of the cup depth may enable the player to surpass this physical limitation.[24]

Throat and Bore

A common misunderstanding of terms centers on the misconception that the "throat" and "bore" are synonymous. The throat actually refers to the area between the cup and the bore, whereas the bore is the narrowest section of the mouthpiece below the throat. Vacchiano suggested that the following points are to be kept in mind when selecting the proper throat and bore: 1) as a cup gets deeper, the throat becomes smaller, 2) as the cup gets shallower, the throat becomes wider, 3) if the student is feeling too much resistance, the throat needs to be widened and 4) a shallow cup by itself will not always give better high notes, but needs to be balanced with the proper-sized mouthpiece bore.[25]

Today, the majority of mouthpiece bores are produced with a stock #27 or #28 standard drill bit size. As the number decreases, the size of the bore increases. For orchestral playing, Vacchiano recommended, as a starting point, a size #23 for a "C" cup on a C trumpet, and a size #21 for the "D" cup on higher pitched trumpets. One must be careful, however, not to open bore too much because intonation, especially above and below the staff, may be negatively affected.

Vacchiano recalled a revelation he had regarding the bore size:

> I think my curiosity about mouthpieces started when I was asked to record the *Magnificat* by Bach. I borrowed a D trumpet and started to practice. I soon discovered I couldn't make the extreme high notes, although I could play them on a regular trumpet. I happened to play a date with Paul Whiteman one day and found out the first trumpet player, Eddie Wade, was playing a mouthpiece with a size #17 bore! He said it was the only way he could get the extreme high notes. After that, I had my answer for the high notes, so I struck a happy medium and settled for a size #21.[26]

Backbore (Venturi)

The backbore, or venturi, of a mouthpiece operates on the principle developed by the Italian physicist, Giovanni Battista Venturi (1746–1822). A Venturi is a system for speeding the flow of a fluid or gas, by constricting it in a cone-shaped tube. In regards to the brass mouthpieces, however, the "Venturi" effect acts in the opposite manner because the air first flows through the smallest part of the taper (bore) and then funnels out through the backbore. The backbore of the mouthpiece is generally measured by the rate and form of taper from the bore to the end of the shank. These customized tapers affect the overall timbre and color of sound. Commercial players most often prefer a small backbore, whereas symphonic players commonly use a larger backbore. Vacchiano recommended the #117 backbore as a good, general backbore for symphonic playing. The Schmidt backbore is typically used with a deep, funnel-shaped cup and is the largest backbore possible. This backbore was originally designed for use with German rotary trumpets. Using a backbore of this size on a piston trumpet, with the other aspects of the mouthpiece out of balance, may create a blunt sound that is too dull.

When finding the right mouthpiece for different pitched trumpets, Vacchiano recommended using a smaller, tighter backbore for the larger horns and a larger, wider backbore for the smaller horns. A small backbore on a large trumpet keeps the sound from breaking up and sounding too labored. A large backbore on a small trumpet creates a bigger and darker sound.[27]

A final point to remember is that any mouthpiece change made in an attempt to improve one facet of playing should not be judged before a ten-day trial. In many cases, it can take six months to a year to fully adjust to a new mouthpiece.

Trumpets in Various Keys

The two teachers who influenced Vacchiano the most with regard to equipment were Georges Mager (with the mouthpiece) and Gustav Heim (with trumpets in various keys). The synthesis of these two teachers made Vacchiano not only a knowledgeable musician, but also one who was well equipped for the rigors of the evolving orchestral music world.

Vacchiano's premise for using a variety of pitched trumpets was to find the trumpet that matched the orchestral style of the composition while being the most efficient with ease of playing. He learned this principle from Heim:

> I studied with Gustav Heim before I came to New York to study with Schlossberg. Heim used to always tell me to use the trumpet that best suited the piece of music. "For instance: if you play *Parsifal*, why kill yourself on a B-flat? Use the D trumpet. If you are playing *Iberia*, use an E-flat. On Schumann's *Symphony No. 2*, I would use an E-flat to make the intonation easier. On the off-stage solo of Mahler's *Symphony No. 3*, the E-flat is ideal. When I played Mozart, I used a special instrument with smaller dimensions; on Wagner I used a big B-flat. On a few

occasions, I even used a low F trumpet that they used years and years ago. The list can go on! I was very successful with this method because I had big trumpets and little trumpets. Because of this, I maintained a collection of about thirty-five different trumpets while I was in the Philharmonic. That was one of the secrets of my success.[28]

Another reason for using differently pitched trumpets is to change the timbre to fit a particular style of music.

Again, on *Parsifal* you don't want to sound clumsy—you want to sound ethereal and using a D trumpet facilitates that much more than a B-flat or C. When you play Tchaikovsky, you want a massiveness and heaviness to the sound, so you use a different horn. When you play the *Circus March* of Ibert, you use yet another trumpet. If you used a large bore B-flat trumpet, you'd sound like an elephant trying to do a dance! This whole concept was one of my biggest fortes.[29]

Vacchiano's consistent drilling of transposition also enabled his students to utilize the higher pitched trumpets without prejudice—the concept was for the student to feel equally at home with any transposition and in any key.

Vacchiano stressed several benefits of transposition:

Many of my colleagues had a very short professional life because they played everything on a B-flat trumpet. By using the proper trumpet, you can make your life much easier and it will add years to your career. The best way to master the different pitched trumpets is to play all your études and excerpts in three keys. After doing this, you will not have any problems changing instruments. Some players say that you should wait until you are older before you start to use these instruments. By that time you might not have a job because you waited too long. When I went to school I used three trumpets every day and played them as much as possible in the school concerts. It's too late to begin when you are out of school.[30]

To prove the point of being comfortable on all the trumpets, Vacchiano periodically told students to close their eyes while he put a trumpet in their hands without their knowing if the trumpet was in B-flat, C, D, or any other key. Vacchiano then instructed: "Play a high G on B-flat trumpet," and while he pressed the appropriate valves, they would hit it every time.

> They didn't know what trumpet I had in my hand but they heard that G and could feel the pressure in the body to make that note come out. You know what makes a person drunk is the imbalance in his ear. It is the same with the trumpet. If he is playing a B-flat trumpet all his life and then you give him another trumpet and he tries to hit the high C like he does with the B-flat trumpet, it's going to cause him a little damage. That's why it's very important that he practice transposition and become comfortable with a variety of pitched trumpets.[31]

Throughout his career, Vacchiano had a tendency to favor the D trumpet, especially on the symphonies of Gustav Mahler. Vacchiano explained his uses of the D trumpet:

> My theory is that someday everyone will be using the D trumpet, with a fourth valve and a very large bell. It is the most perfect instrument. On my recording of Mahler's *Symphony No. 7* with Bernstein, I used a special D trumpet that Vincent Bach made for me. Once you get above the staff (like in the last movement of *Symphony No. 7*), the sound and timbre is much better on a D trumpet than a B-flat. Anyone who doesn't use a D trumpet is a fool.[32]

This theory is especially true for all of the Mahler symphonies that have transpositions in either F or B-flat. If these symphonies were played using a D trumpet, the transposition is either a minor third up or a major third down. Vacchiano's contention was that using a D trumpet in this context gives a more even timbre of sound that is easier to maintain for a sixty-minute major symphonic work.

Choosing the Right Equipment in an Orchestra

The wide variety of trumpets that Vacchiano used in the orchestra gave him the ability to play every composition with ease and assurance. For example, Schumann's *Symphony No. 2* (fig. 6.6) requires the principal trumpet to play a *pianissimo* section that contains several out-of-tune notes on the C trumpet. Vacchiano chose to play this on his E-flat trumpet where these pitches had much more security with the ability to adjust the intonation with the valve slides.

Schumann, *Symphony No. 2*, Trumpet in C

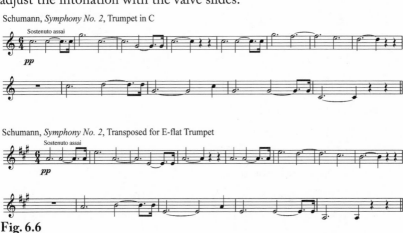

Schumann, *Symphony No. 2*, Transposed for E-flat Trumpet

Fig. 6.6

The aforementioned excerpt relates to the intonation tendencies of the instrument. Other examples address technical issues of fingering and flexibility. "For instance, in the introduction of the [Rimsky-Korsakov's] *Coq d'Or*, I instructed my students to use a D trumpet. This solo is muted so no one can tell the difference, but you and the audience can hear the difference in ease."[33]

Another case where fingering and flexibility are an issue is in Tchaikovsky's *Capriccio Italien* (fig. 6.7) where the cornet solo is in the concert key of D-flat, which is very awkward and risky on a C trumpet. Vacchiano created his own D-flat trumpet, which resulted in a set of fingerings that were much easier and reliable in execution. He did this by removing the tuning slide of his D trumpet and replacing it with the tuning slide from his C trumpet. That combination put the difficult passage in the key of C.

Tchaikovsky, *Capriccio Italien*, Cornet in A

(Transposed for C Trumpet)

(Transposed for D-flat Trumpet)

Fig. 6.7

Donald Green remembered discussing this in his lessons and proceeded to make his own D-flat trumpet:

> I remember Vacchiano telling me about a D-flat trumpet he had. One day I was fooling around on my own, knowing what Vacchiano told me about his D-flat trumpet and you start to see where it would come in handy. I had this old Benge E-flat and the bell had been all beat up. So I took the bell off and I happened to have a C trumpet bell just hanging there. I wondered what key that would put the trumpet in and it put it perfectly into D-flat. So, it is a 239 C trumpet bell on a Benge E-flat chassis. I have used it to record the Bartok *Concerto for Orchestra* (with the LA Philharmonic) and the *Capriccio Italien* (with the Detroit Symphony). There are quite a few places where that horn has come in handy.[34]

The demands of the Philharmonic during Vacchiano's tenure were much different from what they are today. Many times the orchestra recorded during the day, gave a concert in the evening, and then sometimes played it again for the West Coast radio broadcast. This was especially frightening when a piece like Ravel's *Bolero* was scheduled. The ending requires tremendous strength and endurance. Vacchiano played this on his G trumpet so that he could go to a low trumpet for the next piece without much damage. "If I tried to play *Bolero* on a lower instrument, I wouldn't be able to play anything for two days!"[35]

One of the most famous off-stage solos is from Mahler's *Symphony No. 3*. The Philharmonic recorded this in 1961 with Leonard Bernstein. For this recording, Vacchiano decided to have the assistant principal trumpet, John Ware, play the off-stage solo. This is how Vacchiano instructed him:

> I told him exactly what to do. I said, "Look, get yourself the trumpet that's going to be the best in-tune and the easiest to play where you're relaxed. Put a [felt] bag over it and play it out loud and secure. There isn't a fellow in the world who can tell [you are playing a D trumpet] from out in the audience." The conductor never knew and the musicians in the orchestra never knew. In the meantime, he got a wonderful review![36]

In the last few measures of *Ein Heldenleben*, Strauss has written a low F for B-flat trumpet. This note is a half step out of the normal range for B-flat trumpet. It is possible to play it with the valve slides extended, but it is extremely risky, especially at the end of such a demanding piece. Many trumpet players have the trombone play this note for security and then they join in later. To remedy this, Vacchiano invented an extension that enabled him to reach the low F on a B-flat trumpet without the use of slides to make this note more playable. He never again had to ask the trombone player to play it for him.[37]

> I also have a gadget that can put [the trumpet] into a different key. It costs about twenty dollars and has to be made to order to fit your trumpet. You can take the B-flat trumpet, insert the extension into the tuning slide and it lowers the pitch one-third. That makes it a low G trumpet.[38]

Sometimes, conductors get a strange idea and make an almost impossible request of the orchestra. Vacchiano witnessed this on one such occasion with Stokowski:

There was one time when Leopold Stokowski asked me to play the difficult trombone solo from Ravel's *Bolero* on a low F trumpet. Although this part is very difficult on a trombone, it's very easy on a low F trumpet. The low F trumpet wasn't a very practical instrument. The high notes are very difficult to center and very easy to crack.[39]

Even though this request seemed unusual, Vacchiano proceeded to play the solo as Stokowski had requested. If Vacchiano had never played or experimented with a low F trumpet, this would have been much more of a challenge.

Louis Ranger makes the following comment regarding Vacchiano's approach to Weber's *Oberon*:

> Vacchiano taught particular excerpts in the style in which he played them, which was sometimes unusual. For example, in Weber's *Oberon* (fig. 6.8), there is a soft trumpet call. He actually told me to play it with a B-flat trumpet and to remove the second valve slide, finger 2-3 and play it like a bugle call. The result sounds like a very distant cornetto—really, really soft. I just found myself thinking, "Wow, how thoroughly did he have to think this through to come up with that?"[40]

Weber, *Overture to "Oberon,"* Trumpet in D
(play on B-flat Trumpet, remove 2nd valve slide, finger all notes 2-3)

Fig. 6.8

When it came to playing the Classical works of Haydn and Mozart, Vacchiano invented a "mouthpiece mute" that allowed him to play very softly but with great accuracy. This mute is easy to make and actually a rather simple concept. It is made out of a piece of metal called shimstock that is cut with scissors to the length of the mouthpiece backbore. It is then folded around a pencil point and stuck into the backbore of the mouthpiece. Once it is in the backbore, it acts like a spring and will expand inside, thus reducing the size of the mouthpiece's backbore. This, in turn, increases the resistance and only produces about half the volume, but with great accuracy. "It is a great asset to know all these things. The equipment is the number one thing in your study; necessity is the mother of invention. When you have a big job like the Philharmonic, you start to think about how to make life easier."[41]

One must remember that back in the 1940s and 1950s, mutes did not come in as many shapes and sizes as they do today. At that time, no mute played well in all registers and at all dynamics. Vacchiano had the following opinion on the various uses of mutes:

> A good trumpet player always has two mutes: one for high notes and one for low notes. For the high register you want high corks and for low register you want low corks. When my mutes get worn down, I shift them around and use the old ones for low notes and put new corks on the other ones for high notes.[42]

In Shostakovich's *Concerto for Piano, Trumpet and Strings, op. 35*, the trumpet is required to play a muted low F-sharp. The mutes at the time were not suitable for this register, affecting intonation and response. Vacchiano and his former student, Joseph Alessi, Sr., began working on a solution to invent a mute that sounded good in all registers with uniform intonation. After going through almost twenty mutes, Vacchiano and Alessi were not able to improve both the upper and lower registers with the same mute.

One day, Vacchiano accidentally tipped over the shelf containing all of the discarded mutes. While picking them up he decided to try them all again and surprisingly stumbled across one that did exactly what they wanted. The two of them could not understand why they had already discarded the very mute that worked. Upon examining the mute closer, it became apparent that the bottom end of the mute was dented from the fall, changing its shape from a round contour to a flat end as a result of Vacchiano knocking it off the shelf. Thus, the Alessi-Vacchiano Mute was born.[43]

CHAPTER SEVEN

ℛEMEMBERING BILL

✦

Philip Varriale's Eulogy

On September 19, 2005, the music world lost one of its most dedicated students, teachers, and performers: William Vacchiano. After a long battle with various physical ailments, Vacchiano passed away at Cabrini Medical Center in Manhattan from respiratory failure. Philip Varriale, MD, honored Vacchiano's life with this eulogy delivered on September 24, 2005:

On a crisp, sunny autumn day in 1982, I took myself from my home in Westchester and drove to the residence of William Vacchiano. I had never met Mr. Vacchiano, but I had heard a great deal about him as the trumpet icon of the New York Philharmonic and his reputation as a legendary teacher of his time.

I had been sufficiently busy in medical practice as a cardiologist, but my intent was to resurrect my passion to play trumpet after a hiatus of nearly twenty-five years. On arrival, I strolled a short walkway bringing me to the door of a solidly built, two-story brick house in an attractive and well-preserved suburban neighborhood of Queens, New York.

After a cordial greeting by the maestro himself, a tall handsome man with a commanding appearance, I was filled with awe as I was ushered down a stairway into a cozy basement music studio: a well-lit room with two chairs facing a large music stand surrounded by a paneled wall adorned with framed photographic portraits and the Philharmonic Orchestra of an earlier era. One portrait of a man of pleasing appearance with a well-trimmed mustache drew my attention. Mr. Vacchiano proudly pointed to his father, Rafaello, who had arrived at Ellis Island in 1903 from a small village near Naples. On a table nearby sat several trumpets of an older vintage and a large bucket holding a multitude of mouthpieces.

Playing the ubiquitous drills of his hand-written scales and chords, I was put through the paces. Listening and then interjecting his ideas about the proper style of playing and sound, he expounded in the manner of a metaphor and even offered a parable to make his point. "We'll get your feet on the ground," he exclaimed. Translation: to play correctly one must learn and play the fundamentals properly. His style of teaching during the first encounter was vintage Vacchiano—enthusiastic, delightfully folksy, and with a vast experience to share. He was, in short, a musical mensch and a great storyteller to boot.

Within the sanctum of his music room, it was easy to see that Mr. Vacchiano thoroughly enjoyed teaching and was at his best with his students in this one-to-one instruction and time-honored individual lesson. He did not think much of the allure of the seminar or master class, and even less as merit for the serious student. For the multitude of pupils who came to his home for a lesson since he began teaching so long ago, one can fancy a long procession of aspirants who came as pilgrims in search of the Holy Grail.

Mr. Vacchiano (whom I will now call Bill) and I shared a kindred spirit and a bond of deep friendship was forged in a short time. My own family had great affection for Bill and was always happy to see him on his visits to our home in Westchester. My wife, Eileen, and my two sons and daughter always listened with relish and marveled at his quick wit and conversant versatility on almost any topic whether baseball, history, contemporary novels, or even wrestling.

As an avid reader, Bill was a wellspring of far-flung bits of information and became a vicarious contestant when he tuned in to his TV favorites—*Jeopardy* and *Wheel of Fortune*. As a fanatic for the crossword puzzle, Bill religiously worked the puzzle every morning including *The New York Times* puzzle every Sunday.

One summer interlude, Bill joined my family for a vacation at the Gettysburg National Park, the site of an epic Civil War battle. He was thoroughly captivated with the stories of this momentous historical event and filled with great excitement and curiosity during the entire tour of the battlefield, including the celebrated Pickett's Charge.

Bill was especially intrigued with the museum display of brass instruments of the Civil War era. His knowledge of these unusually shaped cornets and saxhorns, mostly pitched in E-flat, was truly amazing. As rudimentary instruments, he was aware of their intonational variance, lack of water keys, and the difficulty of playing period mouthpieces that resembled those used for the modern French horn. During his impromptu commentary, I believe Bill was very much amused by the number of visitors at the exhibit who paused to hear him with the belief that he was our guide.

When he retired in 1973, Bill chose to let the Philharmonic stand as his career zenith, but declined to forfeit his musical heritage and rest on his laurels in a rocking chair somewhere in Florida or even Portland, Maine, where he grew up.

For his new mission in life, Bill would devote himself to teaching both at home and as a denizen professor of trumpet at The Juilliard School, and with time spared to unleash his creative spirits. A written collection of musical ideas and techniques for posterity that would define his approach to his craft became his new goal. With the publication of nineteen books of trumpet methods and études he achieved his magnum opus in hardly more than a decade.

On a typical visit to his home, I would find Bill sitting in his favorite sidearm chair in the corner of his living room writing and reviewing scores of drills and études for a forthcoming publication. A nearby pedestal table was covered with other musical material intermingled with collections of crossword puzzles, mostly complete and perhaps a favorite mystery novel of Agatha Christie. Across the room stood his prize possession, a baby grand piano, dating from his earlier years which he often played while composing his études.

But perhaps most impressive, hanging on the wall above the mantelpiece of an attractive marble fireplace, is a large framed photograph of the Portland Municipal Orchestra circa 1928. A moment frozen in time that captures forever the commencement of a career for Bill Vacchiano who appears as a serious and lanky teenager in the brass section next to his early and revered mentor, Frank Knapp.

On occasion Bill would indulge in an introspective muse and ponder how the fickle finger of fate guided his life. Like many historians whose imagination creates an alternate scenario for an actual historical event, Bill would pose the question, "What if . . . ?"

When the time came to selecting an instrument at the age of nine, Bill was instructed by his father in Italian to select the clarinetto. Confused by similarity of sound, Bill picked the cornetto. In spite of his father's bitter displeasure, his mother sealed his destiny with the remark: "What's the difference . . . leave him alone. He's not going to be a [professional]."

After high school graduation, Bill came to New York to pursue a career as a CPA (as strange as that may seem) and planned to become a student at St. John's University. Walking through Times Square, Bill met an old trumpet friend, Oscar Jones, who suggested a trumpet lesson with the renowned Max Schlossberg. Any ambition for an accounting career was promptly blotted out in the aftermath of that one lesson with Schlossberg and within four years, as his protégé, Bill catapulted his burgeoning career to win a position with the New York Philharmonic in 1935. And it was indeed his destiny to rise to the position of Principal Trumpet and a highly distinguished thirty-eight-year career.

Bill's memory refused to surrender to his age. With astounding quickness, he could call to mind the names of mentors, colleagues, and students of yore and delighted in recounting the anecdotes of his halcyon days with the Philharmonic.

Bill carried his authority and experience with a curious mixture of modesty and pride. On the occasion of his ninetieth birthday in May 2002, Joseph Polisi, President of The Juilliard School, and the brass faculty planned a special celebration for Bill. I recall Bill, in a dry remark to me, wondering whether more than a handful of people would attend. On his day, the Juilliard Board Room was packed with people, pressed together with no space to spare. In this assemblage of colleagues, former students, friends, and family, Bill basked in the glow of their generous good will and was reminded of the rewards they reaped from his priceless guidance, experience, and wisdom.

One year later, not to be forgotten or passed into oblivion, Bill was awarded an Honorary Doctor of Music degree at the Ninety-eighth Commencement Ceremony of The Juilliard School. It was a most spectacular and magnificent event and a presentation to Bill in recognition of a life of great purpose and distinguished musical career.

Like the preacher of routines for his students, it was no surprise that Bill himself was a person of routines and punctual habits. After every lesson in those early days with Schlossberg, Bill would purchase two corn muffins and a cup of coffee from a nearby delicatessen. A distant fifty years removed, Bill resumed that routine and would saunter every morning from his home over two long blocks to a neighborhood bakery to savor a cup of coffee and croissant.

For the many years I knew Bill as a good friend and as his personal physician-cardiologist, I was cognizant of his declining health with his advancing years. Succumbing at first to a life-threatening internal bleed and emergency surgery and, years later, open-heart surgery, Bill's dynamic energy was sapped in no small measure. But Bill resisted the plight of his newer frailties with an indomitable inner strength and did not surrender his zeal for life.

During those last few precious months, Bill was plagued with terrible weakness, a dwindling appetite, and found walking a difficult task. He talked without ease and his voice often strained. He spent his time in a kind of limbo between waking and sleeping and then his grip let loose.

The end-of-life battle did not occur in a vacuum. Most visible in his care was the love, loyalty, and support of his family and friends. The incredible devotion and love of his daughter, Jo Ann, and that of his granddaughters Emily and Jennifer, and good friend Irene—all of whom brought to the bedside every day, a breadth of meaning and comfort for Bill beyond measure.

One may easily proclaim that for years Bill did better than survive—he triumphed. We admire and honor Bill for his abiding passion to perform on the trumpet with a majestically beautiful sound and elegant style and as a teacher who passes his craft to others. When a man's life is over, it should be said that he lived usefully if he was useful to others. For this alone, Bill lived a life of great purpose and achievement. And so, the trumpet shall sound and all of us whose lives he touched for the better—family, colleagues, students, and friends—shall always honor and long remember Bill's enduring musical legacy and friendship and say as he often said, "Thanks a million."

Lee Soper's Memorial

Lee Soper, a former student and friend, spoke at Bill's memorial service at The Julliard School on January 11, 2006.[1]

I've been asked to say a few words about two of the many facets of William Vacchiano. First there is, "William Vacchiano, the Teacher." You've all heard the stories or experienced hours and hours in a small room with a teaching and performing legend. When you think of Mr. Vacchiano's teaching, what is the first thing you probably think of? Mouthpieces, of course. He quite often had three or four mouthpieces on his stand during a concert and would sometimes switch them every other phrase. He loved to experiment with them, but I think the stories of him switching students' mouthpieces are slightly over-exaggerated— just slightly. If you were playing well he probably—most of the time— would leave you alone. But I can quite often remember if you had a bad week he would get that gleam in his eye, reach in his pocket, pull out a mouthpiece and say, "Hey Soper, why don't you try this one." Anyway, it never worked—for me anyway.

The other thing that you think about with Mr. Vacchiano is transposition. Everyone knows that if you took a lesson from Vacchiano you had to know how to transpose. Some may think it was just transposition for the sake of learning how to transpose, but it was much more than that. Mr. Vacchiano viewed transposition as a tool for making music. He looked at it as a way to be comfortable playing a different-keyed trumpet to make a phrase really soar. He wanted us to make beautiful music easily and not have to struggle playing it on the wrong instrument. He also used transposition as a method to train our ears to hear a pitch before actually playing it.

Of course, when you think of Mr. Vacchiano's teaching, you think about rhythm. I can still feel him tapping subdivisions on my arm while I was playing a lesson. Some of the things I vividly remember him saying—and I quite often took notes from lessons. When I would hear a quote, I would go home and I would write it down. But some of the things that I remember most were: "Vibrato shouldn't be artificial. It comes from the heart; it is a reflection of the soul. In fact, all music comes from our soul and is part of our being. Every note that you play should be an extension of the human voice singing to God."

The second, and most important facet of Mr. Vacchiano is simply, "William Vacchiano, the Man." When I think of Bill as a friend, the first word that comes to mind is "gentleman." He was always warm, friendly, polite, and willing to spend time listening to others. He was also very humble. I never saw him take advantage of the fact that he was famous, or be overly impressed with the fact that he was really a legend among trumpet players. Students from around the world came to study with him. Still, he always had his feet firmly planted on the ground.

He did some amazing things musically in his life. Once when we were sitting in the shade of one of our giant pine trees, I asked if he remembered any particularly difficult days performing. He sat there for a second, then smiled and said, "Of course, playing the Bach *Brandenburg*

Concerto on an F trumpet." For those of you who are trumpet players, you know how hard that would be. He sat there for another second and said, "You know, I was a little worried about that one." And, rightfully so.

Also, before the days of digitally splicing in a phrase—or even a note—he told me about recording Stravinsky's *Petrouchka* twice in one day, with two different orchestras and two different conductors, and then playing a concert in the evening. When he told me about that, he modestly said, "Yes, I guess that was a pretty difficult day." I would imagine.

Bill had a wonderfully dry sense of humor. He loved to tease, and when he got that gleam in his eye—watch out. He always seemed to have a positive attitude. Even near the end of his life when he was not feeling well and having difficulty breathing, he tried not to complain. He was at peace with himself and God.

Bill loved coming to our house for lunch or a picnic. We told him that one of our guest rooms was reserved for him and he always asked about "his room." I miss those lazy days of relaxed story telling and his incredible memory. He never forgot a detail; whether it was talking about what the trumpet section had for dinner in 1947 in Raleigh, NC, when they were on tour, or what mouthpiece a student at Juilliard played in 1953. He just had so many stories and he never seemed to repeat one.

We all miss that gleam in his eye. We miss the ease with which he moved comfortably from one new person to another. We miss the fact that he never had a bad thing to say about anyone. We miss his humility. But most of all, we miss him.

Presentation of Honorary Doctorate to William Vacchiano

A prominent member of the New York Philharmonic for nearly four decades and a treasured member of Juilliard's faculty for sixty-seven years, you lay claim to one of the most remarkable careers in the history of American musical performance.

Your exceptional ability as a trumpet player was evident early in your life, while growing up in Portland, Maine. In 1931, you came to New York and entered the Institute of Musical Art—the predecessor institution to The Juilliard School. In 1935, you made history when you won trumpet auditions for positions at the Metropolitan Opera Orchestra and the New York Philharmonic on the same day. Opting for the Philharmonic, you served as assistant principal for seven years and as principal for the next thirty-one, never once missing a concert in which you were scheduled to perform.

A renowned pedagogue, you were appointed to the Juilliard faculty in 1935 and served until your retirement in 2002. In 1995, you estimated that you had taught at least two thousand trumpet students, including such important artists as Miles Davis, Wynton Marsalis, Gerard Schwarz, and Philip Smith. Your students have played in virtually every major symphony orchestra in the country and around the world.

Known for your impeccable technique, beautiful tone, and graceful legato, you are largely responsible for the widespread modern practice of using trumpets in various keys to more closely fit the instrument to the music. You have published numerous trumpet method books and designed your own line of trumpet mouthpieces.

And as a friend and colleague of my father in the New York Philharmonic, you were also caring enough to drive him to the hospital in the middle of a severe snowstorm to see me for the first time on the day of my birth.

In recognition of your extraordinary contributions to the art of music and your years of dedicated service to this institution, Juilliard congratulates you as we award you the degree of Doctor of Music.

Personal Recollections from
Former Students, Colleagues, and Friends

Almost every lesson I had with Vacchiano was on Sunday morning at 11:00 and there was always someone before and after me. I was impressed with how much teaching he did, even on Sundays. At one point during a lesson he went upstairs to take a phone call. While he was gone, I remember counting the number of mouthpieces on his card table as fast as I could—there were 135 of them! If he didn't like how I sounded, he would reach over and grab a mouthpiece from that card table for me to play. Sometimes he would even do mouthpiece modifications on the spot. One time he took a pencil and wrapped sandpaper around the tip and put it in the throat to ream it out a little bit. To tell you the truth, I still play that same Bach 1C he altered in that lesson. I've had it gold plated three or four times since then.

David Baldwin, professor of trumpet,
University of Minnesota
June 16, 2010

He would get you to blow as if you were playing in the Philharmonic—trying to get you to produce that kind of a sound. A lot of us going in at age eighteen or nineteen had no idea if we were making that kind of sound or not. You don't know what it is like to play at that level and what is required of you. That is part of what he was about: training you to get it and to understand that "*This* is forte kid, not that. *This* is the sound you want, *this* is the quality you want, *this* is the attack, length, weight, etc." He wanted it right and he wanted to know you knew what was right. I still remember him poking a pencil into my side as I was playing to make me keep tempo! After I graduated from Juilliard I ran into him at a brass conference and he asked me if I was still playing a 3C. He probably had forty or fifty students between all the schools and he would walk into a lesson and know exactly what was going on—not just your trumpet playing, but your life too. He did what it took to connect with each student, which is the sign of a good teacher. He was an absolutely terrific, wonderful human being and I adored him.

Neil Balm, co-principal trumpet,
New York City Ballet Opera Orchestra
March 19, 2004

Mr. Vacchiano would point out a deficiency in your playing but he would immediately qualify it with, ". . . but there's a cure for that in Arban's, page . . ." In my first lesson, he said, "Whoa, your tonguing is terrible, and the low notes aren't so good either. Don't worry, there's a cure for everything in the Arban's book. Let's get to work." The next lesson, there was a sheet of all articulation studies and two pages of orchestral excerpts that extend to the lower register. He didn't remember my name for the first several times when I started lessons, but he always remembered me by my deficiencies. Our phone conversations went like this:

Me: "Hi, Mr. Vacchiano, this is Michael Blutman."

Mr. V: "Who?"

Me : "Michael. I've taken a few lessons with you recently."

Mr. V: "What did we work on?"

Me: "Articulation and low notes mostly."

Mr. V: "Oh!!! Mr. Low Notes, how are you? Why didn't you just say so?"

For the next several phone calls, I identified myself as "Mr. Low Notes" and he immediately knew who I was.

Michael Blutman,
New York freelance artist
October 24, 2006

I knew Bill as most people did: as a very fine gentleman and a talented musician. Our professional playing careers never crossed paths, but I would indeed consider him a social colleague. He was one of the stalwarts of the legitimate music scene in New York City and everyone admired what he did.

Raymond Crisara, professor of trumpet,
University of Texas at Austin, retired
October 5, 2005

He never spoke an ill word about anybody, and no one ever spoke an ill word about him. He would sit there in Carnegie Hall and watch people argue and wonder why. If there was an argument going on with two other players in the orchestra, he would just lean over to Nat Prager and say, "What is the matter with those two guys?"

Ranier De Intinis, horn,
New York Philharmonic, retired
August 19, 2003

Bill's ego didn't require any kind of feeding. He was a very generous man who didn't need to have his apple polished. In other words, he blew his trumpet, but he never blew his own horn. He only had kind things to say about other principal trumpet players in America. He was a soft, gentle man as a human being and when he played first trumpet he was a monster. I owe my entire career to Bill.

In my second year as his student he finally put things on the table and said very bluntly, "Carm, you're not going to make it because you got bad chops; your lower lip is not good. You're going to have to change your embouchure." Bill handled me like he was remolding me—he just understood. It took a year and a half before I adjusted—it was a horrible transition. I had ten months of torture and he was very helpful every step of the way. He would bring in a dozen mouthpieces at a time with extremely flat rims so that it would grab on my lower lip. Bill Vacchiano gave me high notes. I owe that to him; I owe my job to Bill. If I had not done what he suggested in my second year I never would have been able to play high notes.

Carmine Fornarotto, second trumpet,
New York Philharmonic, retired
September 24, 2003

I was always Bill's last student of the day, so we would walk out to the street together. One day, when we got to Broadway, I wondered why he had stopped. I guess I figured he would have a limousine waiting or look for a taxi. After all, he was principal trumpet of the New York Philharmonic. Pretty soon a bus came along and stopped. He got on the bus, turned, and said, "See you later." I watched him walk to the back of the bus and sit down. I'll never forget it—I just stood there and watched as the bus pulled away with him sitting there in the middle of the back seat, like he was drawn into himself. Had he been going home, it wouldn't have been unusual, but there he was, taking the bus to play a concert that night.

Chandler Goetting, principal trumpet,
Bavarian Radio Symphony Orchestra, retired
September 16, 2003

He was always very concise in his speech. He could say something in two words that takes me five paragraphs to convey to a student. For example, every time I would attack a note, I would move my embouchure. Today, I might stop a student and tell him it isn't good to be moving his embouchure around that much on an attack. Vacchiano simply said, "Don't chew." That's all. It's pretty simple. Consequently, you covered an enormous amount in an hour.

He said to me once, "You know the reason why all you guys make it so easy to teach?" I thought a compliment was coming. He said, "Because you all make the same mistakes. I can tell you where you are going to make a mistake in this next thing before you even start." Actually, that is not surprising, because he taught for so many years. Knowing exactly where the problem points are, which also determines the choice of equipment, is vital. He encouraged self-awareness in knowing exactly where the difficult spot lies.

Donald Green, principal trumpet,
Los Angeles Philharmonic
January 20, 2004

I asked him one time, "Should I take this job?" and he said, "I don't tell anybody yes or no—and there is a reason for that." He went on to explain that in 1940 or 1941 he had a student, [Alexander Nadelson] who asked him, "Hey, I have a chance to play in a Navy band in Hawaii. Should I do it?" and Vacchiano said, "Sure, that'd be great." The guy was on the deck of one of those ships on December 7, 1941, and was killed. Since that time he never recommended a job to anybody. He was very sensitive about that kind of thing. He cared about all of us in a very personal way."

Robert Karon,
Los Angeles freelance artist
January 25, 2004

Mr. Vacchiano's humility and honesty obscured the fact that he was the most influential orchestral trumpet player ever. Just like his small wood-paneled basement studio in Queens, nothing about him was pretentious. His voice, his smile, and his sound all were honest, beautiful, and full of humanity. When I think about all the people he taught, I feel fortunate to have studied with him and I am thankful for the wisdom and knowledge he imparted to me.

David Krauss, principal trumpet,
Metropolitan Opera Orchestra
October 2, 2004

He was like a wonderful Italian grandfather—strict but warm. One time I happened to bring a banana in and I began to snack on it when the lesson ended. He said, "Hey, that looks great." I said, "Oh here, try some." It was so ripe and so perfect that he said, "This is one of the best bananas I've ever had!" So I told my mother about that—I lived at home—and she would pack a banana for him every Monday. One day he took the banana out and sliced it up and put it on a peanut butter sandwich that he had brought with him. He brought the sandwich knowing I'd have that extra banana for him!

Manny Laureano, principal trumpet,
Minnesota Orchestra
July 28, 2003

When I first started taking lessons from Bill, I was also teaching privately in some of the Long Island schools. I was asked to play *Bride of the Waves* at one of the summer community concerts, and I eagerly agreed. I was still a fairly new student with Bill, and in my next lesson I stupidly asked, "I know you're a symphonic trumpet player, but could you help me with this cornet solo?" He said, "Which is it?" So I told him. He sat there and played the whole thing from memory! Incredible!

Albert Ligotti, professor emeritus of trumpet,
University of Georgia
July 20, 2003

For years, I heard people comment on Bill's vivid memory. I never gave it much thought until one day about ten years ago when I witnessed it firsthand. I was playing a concert on Long Island and Bill was in the audience. After the concert, an elderly man approached me and struck up a conversation mentioning that he had studied trumpet many years ago at the old High School of the Performing Arts in the City. I asked if he remembered who his teacher had been. He laughed and said he didn't remember—that it had been almost sixty years ago. I asked if it might have been Bill Vacchiano and he replied that yes, that was his teacher's name, but he hadn't seen him since.

I brought him across the room to meet Bill—the teacher he hadn't seen since high school. He introduced himself and not only did Bill remember him, but also he recalled they had often had lessons in Queens where this student's father owned a restaurant. Bill remembered a sunny afternoon at the restaurant where the two of them had lunch, what they ate, and how they watched the traffic go by on Queens Boulevard from their table. With his lower jaw hanging, Bill's student nodded in agreement as Bill incredibly recounted the details of their day together from over a half-century ago!

Raymond Mase, American Brass Quintet,
Chair of Brass, The Juilliard School
November 4, 2005

On one occasion in the early 1980s, the Canadian Brass was playing a concert at Queens College near Mr. V's house. Ron [Romm] and I invited him to the concert. We picked him up in our stretch limousine. At the concert we paid a tribute to him from the stage and invited him up to play *Bugler's Holiday* with us. Before the concert we had given him the part and he sat for thirty minutes, quietly studying the part without playing it. The piece was programmed near the end of the concert, and he didn't have a chance to warm up when we called him to the stage. The rhythmic intensity was perfect and the notes were solid. This was Mr. V's unmistakable calling card. Perfect!

Fred Mills,
professor of trumpet and brass chamber music,
University of Georgia,
Canadian Brass, retired
August 15, 2003

Over the years we exchanged holiday cards. I would sign mine 2 ½ C. He would then sign 1C under his name. After a matinee at the opera, a friend and I went into Angelo's, an Italian restaurant in New York City. Out of the corner of my eye I saw Bill sitting at a table, and I knew he hadn't seen me come in. I called the waitress over, asked for a piece of paper, and wrote 2 ½ C on it. I said, "You see that man sitting over there? Just go give this to him." Right after, I heard laughter, so I got up and walked toward him. He didn't even see me before he turned and blurted out, "I knew it was you, Bruce!"

Bruce Revesz, second trumpet,
New York City Opera Orchestra, retired
September 9, 2005

For my first lesson, he gave me directions to his house. I drove out to Flushing, and he met me at the door and took me down to the studio in his basement. I pulled out my trumpet and he asked me to play from the Arban book. He had this fan—it was one of those twelve-inch fans that drive you nuts. It drove *me* nuts. The fan broke up my sound, which I was trying to make beautiful. He would say, "Uh, is it a little hot in here? Do you need to sit a little closer to the fan?" I said, "No, no . . . I'm fine." That was my introduction to this very legendary teacher.

One day I got a call from Jimmy Chambers, the personnel director of the Philharmonic, and he asked me to sub for John Ware. It was an all Tchaikovsky concert, Bernstein was conducting, and there was no rehearsal. I called Bill to get some specifics, and he said, "Yeah, we're doing a little Russian music and a couple of other things." He told me to show up at 6:00 P.M. I got there right on time, and there he was—building a trumpet. He finished what he was doing, then he told me that he wanted to play scales for a while, so we did. The concert was at 8:00 and finally, about 7:40 P.M. I said, "I really don't know what the part looks like." He said, "Oh, don't worry about it, let's go—I'll show you the part." He pointed to one part, and said, "I'm gonna lay out here. You play loud as hell." I said, "Okay, no problem." That was my rehearsal!

Ronald Romm, professor of trumpet,
University of Illinois,
Canadian Brass, retired
August 5, 2003

I took my lessons with Mr. Vacchiano on Saturday morning at Juilliard because he didn't teach at the Mannes School of Music building. He never played during my lessons because he always had a matinee that afternoon with the Philharmonic. He always had this B-flat trumpet with him, but never played it. So I asked him why. He just looked at me, then smiled and gave me that famous line of his: "Does Macy's tell Gimbels?"

Now, there's a follow-up to this. Years later, after I had been playing with the National Ballet of Canada, I came back down to New York and I visited Peppy, Bach's old repair man. When I was in the elevator on my way to Peppy's, I heard this gorgeous, rich trumpet sound and the vibrato I knew was his. When I walked in I said, "Hi Mr. Vacchiano. Geez, I thought I recognized that sound from all the way down the hall!" Then he said to me, "Where'd you get that coat?" (I was wearing a long, sheepskin coat with a large collar from Canada.) I said, "Well, does Macy's tell Gimbels?" and he broke up laughing. He had a wonderful sense of humor.

Stanley Rosenzweig, principal trumpet,
National Ballet of Canada, retired
November 23, 2005

I was so excited before my first lesson that I got there early to warm up. I found a room just a couple of doors away from Vacchiano's room, and I warmed up for the better part of an hour. After I walked in, the first thing out of his mouth was, "Was that you playing next door?" I hesitated, not knowing what he would say. "You sound like a bassoon.

When I was your age, instead of warming up so much I would go to listen to recordings of Harry Glantz."

For my second lesson, I spent all week listening to Harry Glantz recordings. This time I had a completely different sound. So I played something out of Saint-Jacome, and he looked at me and said, "What mouthpiece is that?' I said "1¼ C." "Let me take a look at it." He took it out of the horn and gave me this sort of sly smile as he put it in his coat pocket like he was going to take it with him. That was my initiation—from that point on he knew I was serious.

Adel Sanchez, assistant principal trumpet,
National Symphony Orchestra
March 2, 2004

My first lesson with Mr. Vacchiano was a borderline disaster. He took my books from me and said, "Why do you have a new Saint-Jacome's?" "Because you told me to bring it," I said. "No, why do you have a *new* Saint-Jacome's?" he asked. "I didn't have one, so I had to buy it," "You mean you didn't own it?" he asked. "No." He responded, "Yeah, I took a new one into my first lesson with Schlossberg and he thought I was a fantastic reader. He didn't know I had the book memorized." I replied, "You don't have to worry about that with me."

That was the first lesson, but the next four years I spent in Mr. Vacchiano's studio shaped the next forty-plus years of my professional life. In the early years in symphony orchestras, I was playing every piece of repertoire for the first time. If I had any doubts or questions about how to interpret a piece of music, I would first follow the "rules" governing: style, rhythm, and articulation. Then, if I still didn't "get it," I would try to imagine how Vacchiano would sound playing it. The longer I played professionally, the more I appreciated what I had learned in what seemed like an agonizing forty-five minutes a week.

Charles Schlueter, principal trumpet,
Boston Symphony Orchestra, retired
August 7, 2003

I get the most choked up about how Vacchiano was always an inspiration and an encouragement, even decades after his retirement. As I go on in my musical career, I want to be as willing as he was to hand the baton off and be able to do everything I can to lift that person up and say, "Go on, you can do it." We are given that moment to be the best we can and then to encourage others to carry it on and run with it. Bill Vacchiano did just that. He and Julius Baker were both like that to me. They were giants of their time and to hear them say, "You can do this," was tremendous.

Philip Smith, principal trumpet,
New York Philharmonic
August 20, 2003

I collect Civil War cornets and consequently, am familiar with their history and value. One day, when visiting our house, Bill showed me a cornet that he was going to sell and inquired as to what price he should ask. I replied, "Well, Bill, if it's your cornet it's worth more than the going price." He would not hear of that, so we had to totally ignore the fact that his name and fame would add value to the instrument. That is the kind of humility that he was known for. He never took advantage of the fact that he was a living legend among trumpet players.

Lee Soper,
New York freelance artist
October 10, 2003

I have known him over many years and in many different capacities. I knew him as my idol, then as my teacher, then as a colleague at Juilliard, and finally as a close friend. The thing about Vacchiano was that he had a tremendous personality as a player. You heard him play three notes and everybody knew who it was. It was an incredible sound with great personality. I loved the man and just adored him. Lessons were terrific and we had fun together.

Gerard Schwarz,
Seattle Symphony, Music Director
November 12, 2003

After my student days, as a fellow professional, I found Vacchiano to be an affable, warm, and outgoing person who was always a joy to be around; nothing even remotely like his teaching style. He once asked one of my fellow students, "Do you guys ever think of me anymore?" Was he kidding? For my part, there was hardly a working day when I didn't think about him and something he taught me. This is in no way an exaggeration.

Thomas Stevens, principal trumpet,
Los Angeles Philharmonic, retired
August 15, 2003

In 1961 the New York Philharmonic was on tour in Japan and was currently in Tokyo. My friend, an American trumpet player, Dilbert Dale, told me that the Philharmonic had one of the five greatest trumpeters in the world—William Vacchiano.

I looked for him after the concert, and when I found him, he invited me onto the bus. I asked him for a lesson and he said he would return to Tokyo when the tour was finished. We agreed on a date for me to meet him at the hotel. That day, Mr. Vacchiano and Nat Prager were waiting for me in front of the hotel. We went to the hotel café and he ordered each of us a banana split (and told them how to make it). It was my first and it was very delicious. Afterward, we went to his room and he asked me about my studies. He was especially interested in my ability to read music, for he told me Toscanini would "kill" anyone who could not read music well. He demonstrated the different styles that different conductors like Toscanini, Walter, etc. preferred. It was a real eye-opening lesson for me. The orchestra I played with had many guest conductors, but their individual variations were never before explained to me.

My twenty-minute interview with Mr. Vacchiano expanded to over one hour. He recommended several method books for me to study that were unheard of in Japan at that time. He stressed the importance of transposition and suggested I learn to read music in different keys. He recommended Saint-Jacome, Laurent, Chavanne, Clarke No. 3, Goldman's *Practical Studies*, and Walter Smith's *Top Tones*. The books he recommended that day helped Japanese trumpet players immeasurably at that time. He even gave me his own recipe for valve oil. Eventually I asked if he would play something for me, and he chose an excerpt from *Samson and Delilah*. It was a wonderful sound and I wanted more than anything to play that way myself someday.

This first "lesson" was like an epiphany for me. Mr. Vacchiano told me that he listened over and over to recordings of Harry Glantz to get that sound in his ear. Many years later I met Mr. and Mrs. Glantz at the New York Brass Conference for Scholarships. He reassured me that I had done the right thing to come to America to learn the right sound. When I first arrived in New York, Mr. Vacchiano took me to dinner. I remember we had blueberry pie for dessert—one of his favorites. As time went by he became like a father figure to me. I often visited him and "Aunt Jo," as I called Mrs. Vacchiano. I was not only a pupil, but also an honored friend. He was best man at my wedding and, later on, godfather to my two daughters. My good friend lives still in my memory and esteem. I miss him.

Atsuyoshi Takayama,
former student
May 24, 2007

If you had the desire to break into classical music, Bill would find the one thing that would work for each student's needs. Not one student was alike to him. He had an uncanny ability to dig deep in the mind of the student to help that student become aware of his or her capabilities. One of his famous questions to students was, "What is the mother of perfection?" After looking at Mr. Vacchiano thinking the obvious answer was practice, he would come out with the answer, "Repetition!" He inspired me and gave me the confidence to excel as a trumpet player. He was the greatest!

Ronald Tenore,
New York freelance artist
October 18, 2005

Bill's personality and demeanor never changed. He was the same in the orchestra as he was walking down the street. He was just a down-to-earth, friendly person who never said a negative word about anybody in rehearsal or never told any of us what to do. He never raised his voice to anyone; he was always very calm. In my forty years with the Philharmonic, I never saw his temper get involved in a lesson, concert, or rehearsal.

John Ware, co-principal,
New York Philharmonic, retired
March 26, 2004

I think that none of us realized just how unique Bill Vacchiano's teaching was. We assumed, mistakenly, that trumpet students studying with other teachers received similar training in systematic interpretive principles and only later discovered that they did not. Those lessons have been a daily companion in my own work in teaching and playing over the last forty-five years. What came across in his personal relations with his students was enormous caring and kindness. Even though he had a large number of students, he was constantly concerned with our welfare. I know that he thought of us with our individual problems throughout the week and that we were his only concern during our lessons. Often, he would come in and say something like, "I was thinking of your attack this week; I've brought in a mouthpiece that I think will help." If you were having difficulty with transposition, he would bring in his "transposing machine": a set of valves that you could use while reading from the Sachse book in non-playing hours. If you had trouble with the low register, he would bring in his large F trumpet in a cloth bag and loan it to you for a week or two. With all his responsibilities and pressures, how could he give so much concern to his students? I still remember having the feeling in lessons that I was in the presence of a very great artist and one of the most intelligent men I would ever meet. He was truly a great man.

Scott Whitener, professor of music,
Rutgers University
October 6, 2007

Vacchiano was always wonderful to me. When I played first trumpet in the Buffalo Philharmonic (1952–1963), I would go over the next seasons' repertoire with him in the summer and he would clue me in on ways to make the performances easier. He also had a great sense of humor. One time he asked me if I wanted to write down what he had just told me, and the pencil he handed me had a rubber point! I don't know when he slept, because he would have me call him after midnight to arrange a lesson.

Alex Wilson, former principal trumpet,
Buffalo Philharmonic Orchestra
January 27, 2006

APPENDIX A

Principal and Guest Conductors of the New York Philharmonic, 1935–1973

Principal Conductors

1928–1936 Arturo Toscanini

1936–1941 John Barbirolli

1943–1947 Artur Rodziński

1947–1949 Bruno Walter (music advisor)

1949–1950 Leopold Stokowski (co-principal conductor)

1949–1958 Dimitri Mitropoulos

1958–1969 Leonard Bernstein

1969–1970 George Szell (music advisor)

1971–1977 Pierre Boulez

Guest Conductors

Abbado, Claudio

Adler, Peter

Allers, Franz

Ančerl, Karel

Ansermet, Ernest

Autori, Franco

Barati, George

Barenboim, Daniel

Barlow, Howard

Barzin, Leon

Bauer-Mengelberg, Stefan

Beecham, Thomas

Benzecry, Mario

Berio, Luciano

Bliss, Arthur

Böhm, Karl

Bruneau, Alfred

Boulanger, Nadia

Boult, Adrian

Brott, Boris

Brown, Earle
Buketoff, Igor
Burle Marx, Walter
Busch, Fritz
Caduff, Sylvia
Cage, John
Calderon, Pedro
Canarina, John
Cantelli, Guido
Capolongo, Paul
Carvalho, Eleazar
Ceccato, Aldo
Chávez, Carlos
Cleve, George
Cluytens, André
Copland, Aaron
Craft, Robert
Damrosch, Walter
Davis, Colin
De Sabata, Victor
De Waart, Edo
Delacôte, Jacques
Delogu, Gaetano
DePreist, James
Diamond, David
Dixon, Dean
Dufallo, Richard
Ehrling, Sixten
Ellington, Duke
Endo, Akira
Enescu, Georges
Fiedler, Arthur
Foss, Lukas
Frühbeck de Burgos, Rafael
Gamson, Arnold
Ganz, Rudolf
Garcia-Asensio, Enrique
Gielen, Michael
Gilbert, David
Gillessen, Walter
Giulini, Carlo Maria

Golschmann, Vladimir
Goossens, Eugene
Gould, Morton
Hanson, Howard
Harris, Roy
Henderson, Skitch
Hendl, Walter
Herrmann, Bernard
Hindemith, Paul
Houtmann, Jacques
Iturbi, José
Izquierdo, Juan Pablo
Karajan, Herbert von
Katims, Milton
Kaye, Danny
Kertész, István
Kielland, Olav
Kirchner, Leon
Klemperer, Otto
Kondrashin, Kirill
Košler, Zdeněk
Kostelanetz, André
Koussevitzky, Sergey
Krips, Joseph
Kubelik, Rafael
Kurthy, Zoltán
Kurtz, Efrem
Lange, Hans
Leide, Enrico
Leinsdorf, Erich
Levine, James
Lewis, Henry
Lipkin, Seymour
Lombard, Alain
Maazel, Lorin
MacMillan, Sir Ernest
Maderna, Bruno
Maganini, Quinto
Martinon, Jean
McArthur, Edwin
Mechkat, Farhad

Menuhin, Yehudi
Milhaud, Darius
Millar, Gregory
Montemezzi, Italo
Monteux, Pierre
Morel, Jean
Münch, Charles
Ormandy, Eugene
Ozawa, Seiji
Paray, Paul
Pelletier, Wilfrid
Peress, Maurice
Piantini, Carlos
Piastro, Mishel
Previn, André
Previtali, Fernando
Quach, Helen
Reiner, Fritz
Rodgers, Richard
Rosbaud, Hans
Rosenthal, Manuel
Ross, Hugh
Rozsnyai, Zoltan
Rudel, Julius
Rudolf, Max
Sanders, Robert
Sargent, Malcolm
Schelling, Ernest
Schermerhorn, Kenneth
Schippers, Thomas
Schuller, Gunther
Segal, Uri
Semkow, Jerzy
Shanet, Howard
Shaw, Robert
Skrowaczewski, Stanislaw
Smith, Lawrence
Solomon, Izler
Solti, Georg
Springer, Alois
Stanger, Russell

Steinberg, William
Stock, Frederic
Stockhausen, Karlheinz
Stoessel, Albert
Stravinsky, Igor
Thomas, Michael Tilson
Thomson, Virgil
Torkanowsky, Werner
Ustinov, Peter
Van Vactor, David
Villa-Lobos, Heitor
Wallenstein, Alfred
Wyss, Niklaus
Zearott, Michael
Zinman, David

APPENDIX B

New York Philharmonic Trumpet Section,
The Vacchiano Years, 1935–1973

Season	Principal	Second	Third/Assistant	Fourth
1935–1936	Harry Glantz	Nathan Prager	William Vacchiano	Max Schloss-berg
1936–1937	Harry Glantz	Nathan Prager	William Vacchiano	Vacant
1937–1938	Harry Glantz	Nathan Prager	William Vacchiano	Vacant
1938–1939	Harry Glantz	Nathan Prager	William Vacchiano	Vacant
1939–1940	Harry Glantz	Nathan Prager	William Vacchiano	Vacant
1940–1941	Harry Glantz	Nathan Prager	William Vacchiano	Vacant
1941–1942	Harry Glantz	Nathan Prager	William Vacchiano	Vacant
1942–1943	William Vacchiano	Nathan Prager	James Smith	Vacant
1943–1944	William Vacchiano	Nathan Prager	James Smith	Vacant
1944–1945	William Vacchiano	Nathan Prager	Morris Boltuch	James Smith
1945–1946	William Vacchiano	Nathan Prager	Morris Boltuch	James Smith
1946–1947	William Vacchiano	Nathan Prager	Morris Boltuch	James Smith
1947–1948	William Vacchiano	Nathan Prager	Morris Boltuch	James Smith
1948–1949	William Vacchiano	Nathan Prager	John Ware	James Smith
1949–1950	William Vacchiano	Nathan Prager	John Ware	James Smith
1950–1951	William Vacchiano	Nathan Prager	John Ware	James Smith
1951–1952	William Vacchiano	Nathan Prager	John Ware	James Smith
1952–1953	William Vacchiano	Nathan Prager	John Ware	James Smith
1953–1954	William Vacchiano	Nathan Prager	John Ware	James Smith
1954–1955	William Vacchiano	Nathan Prager	John Ware	James Smith
1955–1956	William Vacchiano	Nathan Prager	John Ware	James Smith
1956–1957	William Vacchiano	Nathan Prager	John Ware	James Smith
1957–1958	William Vacchiano	Nathan Prager	John Ware	James Smith

1958–1959	William Vacchiano	Nathan Prager	John Ware	James Smith
1959–1960	William Vacchiano	Nathan Prager	John Ware	James Smith
1960–1961	William Vacchiano	Nathan Prager	John Ware	James Smith
1961–1962	William Vacchiano	Nathan Prager	John Ware	James Smith
1962–1963	William Vacchiano	Nathan Prager	John Ware	James Smith
1963–1964	William Vacchiano	Carmine Fornarotto	John Ware	James Smith
1964–1965	William Vacchiano	Carmine Fornarotto	John Ware	James Smith
1965–1966	William Vacchiano	Carmine Fornarotto	John Ware	James Smith
1966–1967	William Vacchiano	Carmine Fornarotto	John Ware	James Smith
1967–1968	William Vacchiano	Carmine Fornarotto	John Ware	James Smith
1968–1969	William Vacchiano	Carmine Fornarotto	John Ware	James Smith
1969–1970	William Vacchiano	Carmine Fornarotto	John Ware	James Smith
1970–1971	William Vacchiano	Carmine Fornarotto	John Ware	James Smith
1971–1972	William Vacchiano	Carmine Fornarotto	John Ware	James Smith
1972–1973	William Vacchiano	Carmine Fornarotto	John Ware	James Smith

APPENDIX C

New York Philharmonic World Premières, 1935–1973

* Symphony Society of New York
** Stadium Concert
\+ NYP Commission
\++ NYP 150th Anniversary Commission
\+++ NYP Messages for the Millennium Commission
\# Joint Commission

Composer	Composition	Date
Castelnuovo-Tedesco, Mario	*Concerto for Violoncello and Orchestra*	1/31/1935
Barber, Samuel	*Music for a Scene from Shelley for Orchestra*	3/24/1935
McBride, Robert	*Prelude to a Tragedy*	11/20/1935
Saminsky, Lazare	*"Three Shadows," Poem for Orchestra, op. 41*	2/6/1936
Luening, Otto	*Two Symphonic Sketches*	4/11/1936
James, Philip+	*Overture "Bret Harte"*	12/20/1936
Fuleihan, Anis	*Symphony*	12/31/1936
Cella, Theodore**	*Alpine Impressions*	7/26/1937
Purcell-Barbirolli	*New Suite for Strings, Four Horns, Two Flutes, and Cor Anglais*	10/21/1937
Mason, Daniel	*A Lincoln Symphony*	11/17/1937
Read, Gardner+	*Symphony No. 1 in A Minor, op. 30*	11/4/1937
Achron, Isidor	*Concerto for Piano and Orchestra in B flat Minor*	12/9/1937
Porter, Quincy+	*Symphony No. 1*	4/2/1938
Diamond, David**	*Overture for Orchestra*	8/12/1938
Fuleihan, Anis	*Concerto No. 2 for Piano and Orchestra*	12/10/1938
Haubiel, Charles+	*Passacaglia in A Minor ("The Plane Beyond")*	12/18/1938

APPENDIX C

Van Vactor, David +	*Symphony in D*	1/19/1939
Sanders, Robert+	*Little Symphony in G*	2/26/1939
Bonner, Eugene	*White Nights: A Prelude for Orchestra*	4/2/1939
Boyce, William	*Concerto Grosso in D Minor*	4/20/1939
Cesana, Otto	*Three Moods, for Orchestra with two pianos obbligato*	4/22/1939
Bax, Sir Arnold	*Symphony No. 7 in A-flat*	6/9/1939
Bliss, Arthur	*Concerto for Piano and Orchestra*	6/10/1939
Vaughan Williams, Ralph	*Five Variants on Dives and Lazarus*	6/10/1939
Weinberger, Jaromír	*"Under the Spreading Chestnut Tree" Variations and Fugue on an Old English Tune for Full Orchestra*	10/12/1939

Britten, Benjamin	*Concerto for Violin and Orchestra in D Minor, op. 16*	3/28/1940
Fuleihan, Anis	*Symphonie coucer toute for String Quartet and Orchestra*	4/25/1940
Harris, Roy**	*"Challenge, 1940," for Chorus and Orchestra*	6/24/1940
Still, William**	*Ballad Poem, "And They Lynched Him on a Tree," for Double Chorus, Contralto Solo, and Orchestra*	6/24/1940
Schuman, William**	*"This Is Our Time," Secular Cantata No. 1, for Chorus and Orchestra in Five Parts*	7/4/1940
Purcell-Barbirolli	*Chaconne in G Minor, being Sonata #6 from posthumous "Ten Sonatas of Four Parts," originally for 2 violins, gamba, and basso continuo*	10/17/1940
Bach-Barbirolli	*Sheep May Safely Graze*	10/31/1940
Weinberger, Jaromír	*Songs of the High Seas*	11/9/1940

Nabokov, Nicolas	*Sinfonia Biblica*	1/2/1941
Verrall, John	*Concert Piece for Strings and Horn*	1/8/1941
Damrosch, Walter	*"Cyrano" (New Version), Opera in four acts*	2/20/1941
Portnoff, Mischa	*Concerto for Piano and Orchestra*	2/23/1941
Britten, Benjamin	*Sinfonia da Requiem, op. 20*	3/29/1941
Bennett, Robert Russell**	*A Symphony in D for the Dodgers (first concert performance)*	7/30/1941
Still, William	*Plain-Chant for America*	10/23/1941
Smith, David	*"Credo": Poem for Orchestra*	11/8/1941
Smetana-Byrns	*Bohemian Dance Suite*	12/11/1941
Thomson, Virgil	*Suite from the Ballet, "Filling Station"*	12/14/1941
Wetzler, Herman	*Adagio and Fugue from Quartet in C Minor*	12/21/1941
Diamond, David	*Symphony No. 1*	12/21/1941

Chávez, Carlos	*Concerto for Piano and Orchestra*	1/1/1942
Copland, Aaron	*Statements for Orchestra*	1/7/1942
Kurthy, Zoltan	*Scherzo for Orchestra*	1/10/1942
Mohaupt, Richard	*Symphony No. 1*	3/5/1942
Castelnuovo-Tedesco, Mario	*Overture, "King John"*	3/15/1942

Vitoli–Gibilaro	*Chacoune*	3/19/1942
Weisgall, Hugo	*Ballet suite, "Quest"*	3/21/1942
Collins, Anthony	*Overture, "Sir Andrew and Sir Toby"*	3/22/1942
Bach–Barbirolli	*ChoralePrelude, "Wenn wis in hochsten Nothensind"*	4/1/1942
Gretchaninov, Alexandr	*Symphony No. 4 in C Major, op. 102*	4/9/1942
Barber, Samuel	*Second Essay*	4/16/1942
Brant, Henry**	*Variations on a Canadian Theme*	7/11/1942
Dai-Keong, Lee**	*Hawaiian Festival Overture*	7/20/1942
Elwell, Herbert**	*Introduction and Allegro*	7/21/1942
Carpenter, John	*Symphony No. 2*	10/22/1942
Taylor, Deems	*Marco takes a Walk: Variations for Orchestra*	11/14/1942

Corelli–Barbirolli	*Concerto Grosso for String Orchestra in D Major*	2/27/1943
Stringham, Edwin**	*Nocturne No. 2*	6/28/1943
Castelnuovo-Tedesco, Mario **	*American Rhapsody*	8/11/1943
Rogers, Bernard	*Invasion*	10/17/1943
Martinu, Bohuslav	*Memorial to Lidice*	1028/1943
Carpenter, John	*The Anxious Bugler*	11/17/1943
Berezowsky, Nikolai	*Soldier on the Town*	11/25/1943
Herrmann, Bernard	*For the Fallen*	12/16/1943
Taylor, Deems	*A Christmas Overture*	12/23/1943
Berezowsky, Nikolai	*A Christmas Festival Overture, op. 30, No. 2*	12/23/1943
Harris, Roy	*March in Time of War*	12/30/1943

Still, William	*In Memoriam: The Colored Soldiers Who Died for Democracy*	1/5/1944
Hindemith, Paul	*Symphonic Metamorphosis on Themes of C. M. Weber*	1/20/1944
Creston, Paul	*Concerto for Saxophone and Orchestra*	1/27/1944
Schuman, William	*William Billings Overture*	2/17/1944
Rathaus, Karol	*Polonaise Symphonique, op. 52*	2/26/1944
Milhaud, Darius	*Cortege Funebre*	3/23/1944
Lessner, George**	*Puppet Polka*	7/20/1944
Kay, Ulysses**	*Of New Horizons*	7/29/1944
Schenk, Robert**	*Stadium March*	8/13/1944
Strauss, Richard	*Suite from "Der Rosenkavalier"*	10/5/1944
Piston, Walter	*Fugue on a Victory Tune*	10/21/1944
Schoenberg, Arnold	*Ode to Napoleon, op. 41B*	11/23/1944
Wooldridge, John	*A Solemn Hymn to Victory*	11/30/1944

Creston, Paul	*Symphony No. 2*	2/15/1945
Thomson, Virgil	*Symphony on a Hymn Tune*	2/22/1945
Foss, Lukas	*Ode for Orchestra*	3/15/1945
Milhaud, Darius**	*Suite Francaise (Première of symphonic version)*	7/28/1945

Copland, Aaron	*Orchestral Suite from the Ballet "Appalachian Spring"*	10/4/1945
Carpenter, John	*The Seven Ages*	11/29/1945
Milhaud, Darius	*Le Bal Martiniquais*	12/6/1945
Stravinsky, Igor	*Symphony in Three Movements*	1/24/1946
Harris, Roy	*Memories of a Child's Sunday*	2/21/1946
Fitelberg, Grzegorz	*Nocturne for Orchestra*	3/28/1946
Rogers, Bernard	*In Memory of Franklin Delano Roosevelt*	4/11/1946
Jacobi, Frederick **	*Four Dances from "The Prodigal Son"*	7/4/1946
Milhaud, Darius	*Concerto for Cello and Orchestra No. 2*	11/28/1946
Dello Joio, Norman	*Ricercari for Piano and Orchestra*	12/19/1946
Siegmeister, Elie	*"Harvest Evening" (Pt. 2 of "Prairie Legend")*	12/29/1946
Siegmeister, Elie	*Prairie Legend*	1/18/1947
Mennin, Peter	*Symphony No. 3*	2/27/1947
Messiaen, Olivier	*Hymne pour Grand Orchestre*	3/13/1947
Siegmeister, Elie	*Symphony*	10/30/1947
Krenek, Ernst	*Symphony No. 4*	11/27/1947
Gould, Morton	*Philharmonic Waltzes*	11/16/1948
Gibbons-Kay	*Suite for Orchestra*	12/11/1948
Baron, Maurice	*Ode to Democracy (Gettysburg Address)*	1/22/1949
Fitch, Theodore	*Terra Nova*	4/2/1949
Jacobi, Frederick**	*Overture, "Music Hall"*	7/2/1949
Arnell, Richard	*Prelude, Black Mountain, op. 46*	10/29/1949
Dubensky, Arcady	*Concerto Grosso for 3 Solo Trombones, Tuba, and Orchestra*	11/3/1949
Carpenter, John	*Carmel Concerto*	11/20/1949
Ruggles, Carl	*Organum*	11/24/1949
Shulman, Alan	*Concerto for Violoncello and Orchestra*	4/13/1950
Perpessa, Harilaos	*Christus Symphony*	10/26/1950
Babin, Victor	*Capriccio*	11/9/1950
Swanson, Howard	*Short Symphony*	11/23/1950
Ives, Charles	*Symphony No. 2*	2/22/1951
Alexander, Josef	*Epitaphs for Orchestra*	3/8/1951
Koutzen, Boris	*Morning Music, for Flute and String Orchestra*	4/19/1951
Satie-Diamond	*Passacaglia*	10/18/1951
Wolpe, Stefan	*First Ballet Suite, The "Man from Midian"*	11/1/1951
Mills, Charles	*Theme and Variations, op. 81*	11/8/1951
Travis, Roy	*Symphonic Allegro*	12/1/1951

Shulman, Alan	*A Laurentian Overture*	1/17/1952
Kirchner, Leon	*Sinfonia in Two Parts*	1/31/1952
Clapp, Philip	*Symphony No. 8 in C Major*	2/7/1952
Casadesus, Robert	*Suite No. 2, B-flat Major, op. 26*	4/3/1952
Gesensway, Louis	*A Double Portrait*	11/1/1952
Berger, Arthur	*Ideas of Order*	4/11/1953
Rochberg, George	*Night Music*	4/23/1953
Sousa-Gould	*Stars and Stripes Forever*	10/19/1953
Gould, Morton	*Inventions for Four Pianos and Orchestra*	10/19/1953
Gould, Morton	*Dance Variations for Two Pianos and Orchestra*	10/24/1953
Krenek, Ernst	*Concerto for Two Pianos and Orchestra*	10/24/1953
Bezanson, Philip	*Piano Concerto*	11/12/1953
Mohaupt, Richard	*Violin Concerto*	4/29/1954
Dalgleish, James	*Statements for Orchestra*	5/1/1954
Rieti, Vittorio	*Concerto for Violoncello and Orchestra No. 2*	10/28/1954
Harris, Roy	*Symphonic Epigram*	11/14/1954
Rodgers, Richard	*Victory at Sea, A Symphonic Scenario*	11/15/1954
Villa-Lobos, Hietor	*Concerto for Violoncello and Orchestra No. 2, A Minor*	2/5/1955
Gaburo, Kenneth	*On a Quiet Theme*	2/26/1955
Cortes, Ramiro	*Sinfonia Sacra*	4/9/1955
Meyerowitz, Jan	*"The Glory Around His Head," Cantata of the Resurrection*	4/14/1955
Harkness	*Thunderbird (Symphonic Mambo)*	6/25/1955
Barber, Samuel	*Medea's Meditation and Dance of Vengeance, op. 23A*	2/3/1956
Kirchner, Leon	*Concerto for Piano and Orchestra*	2/23/1956
Hall, Reginald	*Elegy for Orchestra*	4/21/1956
Starer, Robert	*Prelude and Rondo Giocoso*	10/27/1956
Rosenthal, Laurence	*Ode*	1/24/1957
Meyerowitz, Jan	*Symphony "Midrash Esther"*	1/31/1957
Gould, Morton	*Jekyll and Hyde Variations for Orchestra*	2/2/1957
Mann, Robert	*Fantasy for Orchestra*	2/23/1957
Kubik, Gail	*Symphony No. 3*	2/28/1957
Sherwood, Gordon	*Introduction and Allegro*	5/5/1957
Foss, Lukas	*Psalms for Chorus and Orchestra*	5/9/1957
Blitzstein, Marc	*Lear: A Study*	2/27/1958
Sicilianos, Yorgos	*Symphony No. 1, op. 14*	3/1/1958
Borishansky, Elliot	*Music for Orchestra*	4/17/1958

133

Gaburo, Kenneth	*Elegy*	4/2/1959
Beglarian, Grant	*Diversions for Orchestra*	4/12/1959
Rorem, Ned	*Symphony No. 3*	4/16/1959
Russo, William	*Symphony No. 2 in C, "Titans"*	4/16/1959
Casadesus, Robert	*Trais Danses, op. 54*	11/5/1959
Schuller, Gunther	*Spectra*	1/14/1960
Luening/Ussachevsky	*Concerted Piece for Tape Recorder and Orchestra (YPC)*	3/26/1960
Bucci, Mark	*Concerto for a Singing Instrument (Concerto for Kazoo), Mvt. III, "Tug of War"*	3/26/1960
Foss, Lukas	*Introduction and Goodbyes*	5/5/1960
Foss, Lukas	*Time Cycle*	10/20/1960
Bernstein, Leonard	*Symphonic Dances from "West Side Story"*	2/13/1961
Weber, Ben	*Concerto for Piano and Orchestra, op. 52*	3/23/1961
Creston, Paul**	*Dance Variations for Soprano and Orchestra, op. 30*	6/20/1961
Diamond, David	*Symphony No. 8*	10/26/1961
Copland, Aaron+	*Connotations for Orchestra*	9/23/1962
Pinkham, Daniel	*Catacoustical Measures*	9/30/1962
Schuman, William+	*Symphony No. 8*	10/4/1962
Milhaud, Darius+	*Overture Philharmonique*	11/29/1962
Barber, Samuel+	*Andromache's Farewell*	4/4/1963
Poulenc, Francis+	*Sept Repons des Tenebres*	4/11/1963
Hindemith, Paul+	*Concerto for Organ and Orchestra*	4/25/1963
Henze, Hans Werner+	*Symphony No. 5*	5/16/1963
Ginastera, Alberto+	*Concerto for Violin and Orchestra*	10/3/1963
Ran, Shulamit	*Capriccio for Piano*	11/30/1963
Wolpe, Stefan	*Symphony No. 1*	1/16/1964
Chávez, Carlos+	*Symphony No. 6*	5/7/1964
Palmer, Robert	*A Centennial Overture*	3/12/1965
Bernstein, Leornard	*Chichester Psalms*	7/15/1965
Cage, John	*Variations V*	7/23/1965
Casadesus, Robert	*Concerto for Three Pianos*	7/24/1965
Ellington, Duke	*The Golden Broom and the Green Apple*	7/30/1965
Ives, Charles	*From the Steeples and the Mountains*	7/30/1965
Wuorinen, Charles	*Orchestral and Electronic Exchanges*	7/30/1965
Schuman, William	*Philharmonic Fanfare*	8/10/1965
Turner, Godfrey	*The Marriage of Orpheus*	3/3/1966
Diamond, David	*Symphony No. 5*	4/28/1966

Diamond, David	*Piano Concerto*	4/28/1966
Webern, Anton	*Kinderstuck, 1924*	7/22/1966
Cowell, Henry	*Hymn and Fuguing Tune No. 16*	10/6/1966
Fuleihan, Anis	*Symphony No. 2*	2/16/1967
Foss, Lukas	*Phorion*	4/27/1967
Hovhaness, Alan+	*To Vishnu*	6/2/1967
Laderman, Ezra	*Magic Prison*	6/12/1967
Schuller, Gunther	*Triplum*	6/28/1967
Rorem, Ned	*Sun, for Soprano and Orchestra*	7/1/1967
Copland, Aaron+	*Inscape*	9/13/1967
Takemitsu, Tōru+	*November Steps*	11/9/1967
Gerhard, Robert+	*Symphony No. 4*	12/14/1967
Nabokov, Nicolas+	*Third Symphony (A Prayer)*	1/4/1968
Shchedrin, Rodion+	*The Chimes ("Zvony"), Concerto No. 2 for Orchestra*	1/11/1968
Bennett, Robert Russell+	*Symphony No. 2*	1/18/1968
Harris, Roy+	*Eleventh Symphony: 1967*	2/8/1968
Hanson, Howard+	*Symphony No. 6*	2/29/1968
Piston, Walter+	*Ricercare*	3/7/1968
Thomson, Virgil+	*Shipwreck and Love Scene (Juan and Haidee) from Byron's "Don Juan"*	4/11/1968
Sessions, Roger+	*Symphony No. 8*	5/2/1968
Schuller, Gunther	*Concerto for Double Bass and Chamber Orchestra*	6/27/1968
Schuman, William+	*To Thee Old Cause*	10/3/1968
Berio, Luciano+	*Sinfonia*	10/10/1968
Walton, William	*Capriccio Burlesque*	12/7/1968
Babbitt, Milton+	*Relata II*	1/16/1969
Kirchner, Leon+	*Music for Orchestra*	10/16/1969
Schuman, William	*In Praise of Shahn, Canticle for Orchestra*	1/29/1970
Carter, Elliott+	*Concerto for Orchestra*	2/5/1970
Hovhaness, Alan	*And God Created Great Whales*	6/11/1970
Stockhausen, Karlheinz+	*Hymnen*	2/25/1971
Nash, Ogden	*Carnival of Marriage*	6/2/1971
Copland, Aaron	*Three Latin American Sketches*	6/7/1972
Berio, Luciano+	*Concerto for Two Pianos and Orchestra*	3/15/1973

APPENDIX D

New York Philharmonic U.S. Premières, 1935–1973

* Symphony Society of New York
** Stadium Concert
+ NYP Commission

Composer	Composition	Date
Delius, Frederick	*"Koanga," Dance*	1/2/1936
Delius, Frederick	*"Koanga," Finale*	1/12/1936
Verdi, Giuseppe	*String Quartet in E Minor*	1/23/1936
Bax, Sir Arnold	*The Tale the Pine Trees Knew*	11/5/1936
Purcell-Barbirolli	*Suite for Strings*	11/7/1936
Vaughan Williams, Ralph	*"Job," A Masque for Dancing*	11/26/1936
Barbirolli, John	*Oboe Concerto on Themes of Pergolesi*	1/6/1937
Jora, Mihail	*Marche Juive*	1/28/1937
Otesco, Nonna	*"De La Matei Citire," Prelude to Act II*	1/30/1937
Bartok, Béla	*Music for Strings, Percussion and Celesta*	10/28/1937
Rossellini, Renzo**	*Canto di Palude*	7/18/1938
Castelnuovo-Tedesco, Mario**	*Overture to "The Merchant of Venice"*	6/18 /1939
Rossellini, Renzo**	*Prelude to "Aminta"*	6/24/1939
Gomez, Carlos**	*Suite Andaluza*	7/15/1939
Aguirre, Julián **	*"Huella y Gato" from Two Argentine Dances*	7/19/1939
Johnson, Horace**	*The Streets of Florence*	7/19/1940
Zemlinsky, Alexander	*Sinfonietta for Orchestra, op. 23*	12/29/1940

Miaskovsky, Nikolay	*Violin Concerto*	3/1/1941
Montemezzi, Italo	*Paolo e Virginia*	3/6/1941
Benjamin, Arthur**	*Cotillon*	6/20/1941
Sanjuán, Pedro**	*"Iniciacion" from Liturgia Negra*	6/24/1941
Walton, William**	*Crown Imperial (Coronation March)*	7/14/1941
Mendelssohn-Stewart**	*Fugue in E Minor*	7/16/1941
Khachaturian, Aram**	*Symphony*	7/10/1942
Khachaturian, Aram**	*Allegro and Dance Lesguine (Presto) from "Dance Suite"*	7/20/1942
Miaskovsky, Nikolay	*Symphony No. 21*	11/5/1942
Bartok, Béla	*Concerto for Two Pianos and Orchestra*	1/21/1943
Bate, Stanley	*Concertante for Piano and String Orchestra*	1/30/1943
Ireland, John	*Epic March*	2/18/1943
Miaskovsky, Nikolay**	*Symphony No. 16*	7/3/1943
Shostakovich, Dmitry	*Symphony No. 8, op. 65*	4/2/1944
Vaughan Williams, Ralph	*Symphony No. 5, D Major*	11/30/1944
Villa-Lobos, Heitor	*Choros No. 9*	2/8/1945
Stolz, Robert**	*L'Heure Bleu*	8/6/1945
Stolz, Robert**	*Turkish March*	8/6/1945
Prokofiev, Sergey	*A Summer Day, op. 65*	10/25/1945
Ibert, Jacques	*Festival Overture*	3/28/1946
Rosenthal, Manuel	*Musique de Table*	10/10/1946
Rosenthal, Manuel	*La Fete du Vin*	12/5/1946
Barraud, Henry	*Piano Concerto*	12/5/1946
Lully-Rosenthal	*Noce Villageoise*	12/5/1946
Pinto, Octavio	*Scenas Infantis (Children's Scenes)*	1/4/1947
Honegger, Arthur	*Symphony No. 3 ("Symphonie Liturgique")*	1/23/1947
Mahler, Gustav	*Symphony No. 6, A Minor*	12/11/1947
Honegger, Arthur	*Jeanne D'Arc au Bucher*	1/1/1948
Khachaturian, Aram	*Russian Fantasy*	4/1/1948
Perpessas, Harilaos	*Prelude and Fugue for Orchestra*	11/4/1948
Rathaus, Karol	*Vision Dramatique*	11/18/1948
Honegger, Arthur	*Symphony No. 4 ("Deliciae Basilienses")*	12/30/1948
Moeran, Ernest	*In the Mountain Country*	1/27/1949
Dyson, George	*Overture to "Canterbury Pilgrims"("At the Tabard Inn")*	2/10/1949

Palau Boix, Manuel**	*Marcha burlesque*	7/4/1949
López-Chavarri Marco, Eduardo**	*Cradle Song*	7/4/1949
López-Chavarri Marco, Eduardo**	*Popular Valencian Dance*	7/4/1949
Balendonck, Armand**	*"Cosmos" Ballet Scene*	7/6/1949
Miaskovsky, Nikolay	*Slavonic Rhapsody, op. 71*	10/20/1949
Porrino, Ennio	*Sardegna*	11/5/1949
Ivanov-Radkevich	*Russian Overture*	11/13/1949
Aubert, Jacques	*Offrande*	11/17/1949
Prokofiev, Sergey	*Symphony No. 6, op. 111*	11/24/1949
Schumann, Robert	*Introduction and Concert-Allegro, op. 134*	11/13/1950
Martin, Frank	*Concerto for 7 Wind Instruments*	12/28/1950
Malipiero, Gian	*Piano Concerto No. 4*	3/29/1951
Busoni, Ferruccio	*Arlecchino (concert version)*	10/11/1951
Schoenberg, Arnold	*"Erwartung" ("Expectation"), Monodrama, op. 17*	11/15/1951
Rivier, Jean	*Piano Concerto No. 1, C Major*	3/6/1952
Milhaud, Darius	*Christopher Columbus (concert version)*	11/6/1952
Martin, Frank	*Violin Concerto*	11/13/1952
Ferguson, Howard	*Piano Concerto, D Major*	2/5/1953
Eberl, Anton	*Symphony, C Major*	3/12/1953
Ghedini, Giorgio	*Concerto of the Albatross*	3/19/1953
Pizzetti, Ildebrando	*Preludio a un Altro Giorno*	3/26/1953
Giovanni-Ghedini	*La Battaglia*	3/26/1953
Einem, Gottfried von	*Orchestermusik, op. 9*	4/16/1953
Einem, Gottfried von	*Capriccio, op. 2*	10/15/1953
Malipiero, Gian	*Vivaldiana*	10/22/1953
Blacher, Boris	*Ornaments*	11/19/1953
Haydn, Joseph	*Overture for an English Opera*	11/19/1953
Bach-Webern	*Musical Offering, Ricercare No. 2*	11/29/1953
Falla, Manuel de	*Homages*	2/18/1954
Shostakovich, Dmitry	*Symphony No. 10, op. 93*	10/14/1954
Skalkottas, Nikos	*Greek Dances*	11/4/1954
Marinuzzi, Gino	*Fantasia Quasi Passacaglia*	1/13/1955
Bonporti, Francesco	*Concerto Grosso No. 8, D Major, op. 11*	1/13/1955
Ladmirault, Paul	*Variations Sur Des Airs De Biniou*	4/2/1955
Lehar, Franz**	*Overture to "The Merry Widow"*	7/21/1955
Wagenaar, Bernard	*Five Tableaux for Violoncello*	12/8/1955
Shostakovich, Dmitry	*Violin Concerto No. 1, op. 99, (op. 77)*	12/291955

Chávez, Carlos	*Symphony No. 3*	1/26/1956
Liebermann, Rolf	*Musique*	2/25/1956
Prokofiev, Sergey	*Sinfonia Concertante, op. 125, (Cello Concerto No. 2)*	4/19/1956

Copland, Aaron	*Symphony No. 2 ("Short Symphony")*	1/24/1957
Prokofiev, Sergey	*The Ugly Duckling (rev. edition)*	2/16/1957
Schuller, Gunther	*Dramatic Overture*	3/7/1957
Egge, Klauss	*Violin Concerto, op. 26*	4/27/1957
Bentzon, Niels Viggo	*Variazioni Brevi, op. 75*	5/9/1957
Villa-Lobos, Heitor**	*Preludio Sinfonico, from the Opera "Izart"*	7/8/1957
Villa-Lobos, Heitor**	*Fantasy for Cello and Orchestra*	7/8/1957
Bloch, Ernest**	*Lady Macbeth's Sleepwalking Scene (from "Macbeth")*	7/17/1957
Kabalevsky, Dmitry	*Symphony No. 4*	10/31/1957
Bondeville, Emmanuel	*Symphonie Lyrique*	11/16/1957
Rota, Nino	*Variazioni Sopra un Tema Gioviale*	12/12/1957

Shostakovich, Dmitry	*Piano Concerto No. 2, op. 102*	1/2/1958
Markevitch, Igor	*Icare*	4/10/1958
Castro, Juan José	*Corales Criollos*	3/20/1958
Zafred, Mario	*Symphony No. 4 ("In Honor of the Resistance")*	10/30/1958

| Ben-Haim, Paul | *The Sweet Psalmist of Israel* | 4/23/1959 |
| Starer, Robert | *Concerto for Viola, Strings and Percussion* | 12/10/1959 |

| Amirov, Fikret | *Symphonic Suite (Azerbaijan)* | 3/3/1960 |
| Boulez, Pierre | *Improvisations sur Mallarme* | 3/31/1960 |

Tansman, Alexandre	*Suite Baroque*	2/23/1961
Villa-Lobos, Heitor	*Sinfonia de Paz*	3/5/1961
Villa-Lobos, Heitor	*Madonna Tone Poem*	3/5/1961
Boulez, Pierre	*Improvisations sur Mallarme, No. 2*	3/16/1961
Brahms-Sargent**	*Four Serious Songs, op. 121*	7/26/1961

| Etler, Alvin | *Wind Quintet Concerto (1960)* | 10/25/1962 |

| Gerhard, Roberto | *Symphony No. 1* | 1/10/1963 |
| Baird, Tadeusz | *Four Essays for Orchestra* | 11/28/1963 |

Ligeti, György	*Atmospheres*	1/2/1964
Xenakis, Iannis	*Pithoprakta*	1/2/1964
Brown, Earle	*Available Forms 2*	2/6/1964

Messiaen, Olivier	*Chronochromie: Strophe et Antistrophe*	7/24/1965
Webern, Anton	*String Trio, 1925*	7/22/1966
Blomdahl, Karl-Birger	*Forma Ferritonans*	3/9/1967
Shostakovich, Dmitry	*Violin Concerto No. 2, op. 126*	1/11/1968
Mitropoulos, Dimitri	*Concerto Grosso for Orchestra*	3/14/1968
Stockhausen, Karlheinz	*Hymnen (Religion I and II)*	2/25/1971
Stockhausen, Karlheinz	*Hymnen (Religion IV)*	2/25/1971
Pousseur, Henri	*Couleurs Croisees*	5/13/1971
Paganini, Nicolò	*Violin Concerto No. 4, D Minor*	8/20/1971
Maderna, Bruno	*Violin Concerto*	1/20/1972
Dvořák, Antonín	*Symphony No. 1, C Minor, op. 3 ("Bells...")*	12/1/1972

APPENDIX E

Selected Discography of
William Vacchiano with the
New York Philharmonic, 1935–1973

(Excerpted from the New York Philharmonic Archives Discography)[1]

Composer	Composition (Conductor)	Recording Date and Albums
Bach, J.S.	*Magnificat in D Major, BWV 243* (Bernstein)	2/18/1959 LPs: MS-6375, ML-5775, BOM-517554 CDs: SBK-60261
Bartok, Béla	*Concerto for Orchestra* (Bernstein)	11/30/1959 LPs: MS-6140, ML-5471 CDs: MK-44707, SMK-47510, SMK-60730
Bartok, Béla	*Concerto for Orchestra* (Boulez)	12/18/1972 LPs: M-32132, MQ-32132, MY-37259, HM-42132 CDs: MYK-37259, MK-42397
Bartok, Béla	*The Miraculous Mandarin* (Boulez)	5/11/1971 LPs: M-31368, MQ-31368 CDs: SMK-45837
Beethoven, Ludwig van	*Leonore Overture No. 2* (Walter)	Unknown LPs: P-15441(e)

Beethoven, Ludwig van	*Leonore Overture No. 3, op. 72a* (Bernstein)	10/24/1960 LPs: MS-6223, ML-5623, M-30079, M-31071, M3X-31068 CDs: MK-42222, SMK-47521, SMK-63153
Beethoven, Ludwig van	*Leonore Overture No. 3, op. 72a* (Walter)	12/6/1954 LPs: ML-5232, ML-5368 CDs: SMK-64487, SX9K-66249
Beethoven, Ludwig van	*Symphony No. 9 in D Minor, op. 125* (Bernstein)	5/19/1964 LPs: M2S-794, D8S-815 CDs: MK-42224, SMK-47518, SMK-63152
Beethoven, Ludwig van	*Symphony No. 9 in D Minor, op. 125* (Walter)	4/16/1949 LPs: SL-56, SL-156 (with 1949 finale), SL-186, A-1067(EP), ML-5200, 32-66-0001, 32-16-0322(e) (with 1953 finale) CDs: MPK-45552 (with 1953 finale)
Berg, Alban	*Wozzeck* (Mitropoulos)	4/12/1951 LPs: SL-118, Y2-33126, M2P-42470 CDs: MH2K-62759
Berlioz, Hector	*Symphony Fantastique, op. 14* (Bernstein)	5/27/1964 LPs: MS-6607, ML-6007 CDs: SMK-47525, SMK-60968
Berlioz, Hector	*Symphony Fantastique, op. 14* (Bernstein)	3/5/1968 LPs: MS-7278, M-31843, MY-38475 CDs: MYK-38475
Brahms, Johannes	*Symphony No. 1 in C Minor, op. 68* (Walter)	12/30/1953 LPs: SL-200, DSL-200, ML-5124, 32-36-0007

Brahms, Johannes	*Symphony No. 2 in D Minor, op. 73* (Bernstein)	5/29/1962 LPs: MS-6374, ML-5774, D3M-32097 CDs: SMK-47537, SMK-61829
Brahms, Johannes	*Symphony No. 2 in D Minor, op. 73* (Walter)	12/28/1953 LPs: SL-200, DSL-200, ML-5125, 32-36-0007
Brahms, Johannes	*Symphony Nos. 2 and 3: Rehearsal Excerpts* (Walter)	12/18–28/1953 LPs: Lp-32785/86, included in SL-200 and DSL-2000, boxed sets of Brahms Symphonies.
Brahms, Johannes	*Symphony No. 3 in F Major, op. 90* (Walter)	12/21,23/1953 LPs: Lp-32785/86, included in SL-200 and DSL-2000, boxed sets of Brahms Symphonies.
Brahms, Johannes	*Symphony No.4 in E Minor, op. 98* (Bernstein)	10/9/1962 LPs: MS-6479, ML-5879, D3M-32097 CDs: SMK-47538, SMK-661846
Brahms, Johannes	*Symphony No. 4 in E Minor, op. 98* (Walter)	2/12/1951 LPs: ML-4472, A-1090(EP), SL-200, DSL-200, ML-5127, 32-36-0007
Britten, Benjamin	*Variations and Fugue on a Theme of Purcell, op. 34, "The Young Person's Guide to the Orchestra"* (Bernstein)	3/20/1961 LPs: MS-6368, ML-5768, M-31808, D3S-785 CDs: SFK-46712, SMK-60175
Bruckner, Anton	*Symphony No. 9 in D Minor* (Bernstein)	2/4/1969 LPs: M-30828 CDs: SMK-47542
Carter, Elliott	*Concerto for Orchestra* (Bernstein)	2/11/1970 LPs: M-30112, CRI SD-469 CDs: SMK-60203

Copland, Aaron	*An Outdoor Overture* (Bernstein)	11/12/1960 CDs: NYP-2012 in set NYP-2003/13
Copland, Aaron	*Billy the Kid: Prairie Night and* *Celebration Night* (Stokowski)	11/3/1947 78s: 19011-D LPs: ML-2167, A-1516(EP)
Copland, Aaron	*Billy the Kid: Suite* (Bernstein)	10/20/1959 LPs: MS-6175, ML-5575, M-50155, M-31823, MY-36727, MG-30071, P-18865 CDs: MYK-36727, MK-42265, SMK-47543, SMK-63082
Copland, Aaron	*Connotations for Orchestra* (Bernstein)	9/23/1962 LPs: L2S-1008, L2L-1007, MS-7431 CDs: SM2K-47236, SMK-60177
Copland, Aaron	*El Salon México* (Bernstein)	5/20/1961 LPs: MS-6355, ML-5755, MS-6441, ML-5841, MS-7521, MG-30071, MY-37257, M-39443, MGP-13 CDs: MYK-37257, SMK-47544, SMK-60571, SFK-89274
Copland, Aaron	*Fanfare for the Common Man* (Bernstein)	2/16/1966 LPs: MY-37257 CDs: MYK-37257, MK-42265, MLK-44723, SFK-46715, SMK-47543, SMK-63082, SMK-64075
Copland, Aaron	Four Dance Episodes from *Rodeo* (Bernstein)	5/2/1960 LPs: MS-6175, ML-5575, MG-30071, M-31823, MY-36727 CDs: MYK-36727, MK-42265, SMK-47543, SMK-63082, Smithsonian RD 103-4

Copland, Aaron	*Lincoln Portrait* (Kostelanetz)	3/15/1958 LPs: MS-6040, ML-5347, CSP-91A02007 CDs: SM2K-89326
Copland, Aaron	*Symphony for Organ and* *Orchestra* (Bernstein)	1/3/1967 LPs: MS-7058, ML-6458 CDs: SM2K-47232, SMK-63155
Copland, Aaron	*Third Symphony* (Bernstein)	2/16–17/1966 LPs: MS-6954, ML-6354 CDs: SMK-63155
Debussy, Claude	*La Mer* (Bernstein)	10/16/1961 LPs: MS-6754, ML-6154 CDs: SMK-47546, SMK-60972
Debussy, Claude	*La Mer* (Walter)	1/19/1941 LPs: NYP-84 1/2
Debussy, Claude	*Nocturnes: Fêtes* (Bernstein)	9/28/1960 LPs: MS-6271, ML-5671 CDs: SMK-47546, SMK-60972
Dvořák, Antonín	*Symphony No. 9 in E Minor, op.* *95, "from the New World"* (Bernstein)	4/16/1962 LPs: MS-6393, ML-5793, D3S-737, D3L-337, M-31809 CDs: SMK-47547, SMK-60563
Gershwin, George	*An American in Paris* (Bernstein)	12/15/1958 LPs: MS-6091, ML-5413, M-31804, MY-37242, MG- 31155, FM-42516 CDs: MYK-37242, MK-42264, MK-42516, SFK-46715, SMK-47529, SMK-63086

Gershwin, George	*Concerto in F* (Oscar Levant, piano) (Kostelanetz)	5/4/1942 78s: 11818/21-D in set M-512, 11822/25-D in set MM-512 LPs: ML-4025, A-1047(EP), ML-4879, CL-700, CS-8641e, FM-42514 CDs: MK-42514, MPK-47681
Händel, G. F.	*Messiah, HWV 56* (Bernstein)	12/31/1956 LPs: MS-6038/39 in set M2S-603, ML-5023/24 in set M2L-242, MS-6020, ML-5300, MS-6041, ML-5346, MS-6928, ML-6328, MY-38481 CDs: SM2K-60205
Hindemith, Paul	*Concert Music for Brass and Strings, op. 50* (Bernstein)	5/13/1961 LPs: MS-6579, ML-5979 CDs: SMK-47566
Hindemith, Paul	*Symphonic Metamorphosis on Themes of C. M. von Weber* (Bernstein)	1/16/1968 LPs: MS-7426, MP-38754 CDs: SMK-47566
Hindemith, Paul	*Symphony: Mathis der Maler* (Bernstein)	12/23/1956 CDs: NYP-2005 in set NYP 2003/13
Holst, Gustav	*The Planets, op. 32* (Bernstein)	11/30/1971 LPs: M-31125, MQ-31125, MY-37226 CDs: MYK-37226, SMK-47567, SBK-62400, SMK-63087
Ives, Charles	*The Unanswered Question* (Bernstein)	4/17/1964 LPs: MS-6843, ML-6243, M4-32504, M3X-33028, MP-38777 CDs: MK-42407, SFK-46701, SMK-60203
Kodály, Zoltán	*Háry János: Suite* (Mitropoulos)	2/27/1956 LPs: ML-5101, P-14202e

Mahler, Gustav	*Das Lied von der Erde* (Walter)	1/18/1948 CDs: NYP-9808 in set NYP-9801+12 (12 CDs)
Mahler, Gustav	*Das Lied von der Erde* (Walter)	4/18, 5/1960 LPs: M2S-617, M2L-255, MS-6426, ML-5825, Y-30043, D3S-744, D3L-344, MP-39027 CDs: MK-42034, MYK-45500, SMK-64455, SX10K-66246
Mahler, Gustav	*Symphony No. 1 in D Major* (Walter)	1/25/1954 LPs: SL-218, ML-4958 CDs: MHK-63328
Mahler, Gustav	*Symphony No. 1 in D Major* (Barbirolli)	1/10/1959 CDs: NYP-9801 in set NYP-9801+12 (12 CDs)
Mahler, Gustav	*Symphony No. 1 in D Major* (Bernstein)	10/4/1966 LPs: GMS-765, MS-7069, M4X-31427, M-31834 CDs: MK-42194, SM2K-47573, SMK-60732
Mahler, Gustav	*Symphony No. 2 in C Minor* (Walter)	2/18/1957 2/17, 21/1958 LPs: M2S-601, M2L-256, Y2-30848, M3P-39635 CDs: M2K-42032, MB2K-45674, SM2K-64447, SX10K-66246
Mahler, Gustav	*Symphony No. 2 in C Minor* (Bernstein)	9/29, 30/1963 LPs: M2S-695, M2L-295, GMS-765, M4X-31432 CDs: SM2K-63159
Mahler, Gustav	*Symphony No. 3 in D Minor* (Bernstein)	4/3/1961 LPs: M2S-675, M2L-275, GMS-765, M4X-31432 CDs: M2K-42196, SM2K-47576, SM2K-61831

Mahler, Gustav	*Symphony No. 4 in G Major* (Walter)	5/10/1945 LPs: ML-4031, 32-16-0025 CDs: MPK-46450, SMK-64450, SX10K-66246
Mahler, Gustav	*Symphony No. 4 in G Major* (Bernstein)	2/1/1960 LPs: MS-6152, ML-5485, GMS-765, M3X-31437 CDs: SMK-47579, SMK-60733
Mahler, Gustav	*Symphony No. 4 in G Major* (Solti)	1/13/1960 CDs: NYP-9804 in set NYP- 9801+12 (12 CDs)
Mahler, Gustav	*Symphony No. 5 in C-sharp* *Minor* (Walter)	2/10/1947 78s: 12683/90-D in set M-718, 12666/73-D in set MM-718 LPs: SL-171, 32-26-0016 CDs: MPK-47683, SMK-64451, SX10K-66246
Mahler, Gustav	*Symphony No. 5 in C-sharp* *Minor* (Mitropoulos)	1/3/1960 LPs: NYP-81 1/2
Mahler, Gustav	*Symphony No. 5 in C-sharp* *Minor* (Bernstein)	1/7/1963 LPs: M2S-698, M2L-298, GMS-765, M3X-31437 CDs: MK-42198, SMK-47580, SMK-63084
Mahler, Gustav	*Symphony No. 6 in A Minor* (Bernstein)	5/2, 6/1967 LPs: GMS-765, M3S-776, M4X-31427 CDs: M3K-42199, SM3K-47581, SMK-60208
Mahler, Gustav	*Symphony No. 7 in E Minor* (Bernstein)	12/14–15/1965 LPs: M2S-739, M2L-339, GMS-765, M4X-31441 CDs: M3K-42200, SM3K-47585, SMK-60564

Mahler, Gustav	*Symphony No. 8 in E-flat Major* (Stokowski)	4/9/1950 CDs: NYP-9809 in set NYP-9801+12 (12 CDs)
Mahler, Gustav	*Symphony No. 9 in D Major* (Barbirolli)	12/8/1962 CDs: NYP-9810 in set NYP-9801+12 (12 CDs)
Mahler, Gustav	*Symphony No. 9 in D Major* (Bernstein)	12/16/1965 LPs: GMS-765, M3S-776, M4X-31427 CDs: M3K-42200, SM3K-47585, SMK-60597
Mahler, Gustav	*Symphony No. 10 in F-sharp Minor: Purgatorio* (Mitropoulos)	3/16/1958 CDs: NYP-9811 in set NYP-9801+12 (12 CDs)
Mahler, Gustav	*Symphony No. 10 in F-sharp Minor: Andante-Allegro* (Mitropoulos)	1/16/1960 CDs: NYP-9811 in set NYP-9801+12 (12 CDs)
Meyerbeer, Giacomo	*La Prophéte: Coronation March, Act 3* (Bernstein)	10/26/1967 LPs: MS-7271, MG-35919 CDs: MLK-44723, MDK-45734, SMK-63154, SMK-64075
Mussorgsky, Modest	*Pictures at an Exhibition (Ravel)* (Bernstein)	10/14/1958 LPs: MS-6080, ML-5401, MY-36726 CDs: MYK-36726, SMK-47595, SMK-60693
Mussorgsky, Modest	*Pictures at an Exhibition (Ravel)* (Rodziński)	3/12/1945 78s: 12421/24-D in set M-641, 12425/28-D in set MM-641 LPs: ML-4033, RL-3119, HL-7075
Mussorgsky, Modest	*Pictures at an Exhibition (Ravel)* (Schippers)	1/11/1965 LPs: 32-11-0012, 32-11-00115, 32-16-0376

Nielsen, Carl	*Symphony No. 4, op. 29* (Bernstein)	2/9/1970 LPs: M-30293, M3P-39639 CDs: S4K-45989, SMK-47597
Nielsen, Carl	*Symphony No. 5, op. 50* (Bernstein)	4/9/1962 LPs: MS-6414, ML-5814 CDs: MK-44708, S4K-45989, SMK-47598
Prokofiev, Sergey	*Lieutenant Kijé Suite, op. 60* (Mitropoulos)	1/9/1956 LPs: ML-5101, P-14202e
Prokofiev, Sergey	*March for Band, op. 99* (Kurtz)	4/20/1946 78s: 12881-D LPs: ML-4233
Prokofiev, Sergey	*Peter and the Wolf, op. 67* (Bernstein)	2/16/1960 LPs: MS-6193, ML-5593, D3S-785, CC-25501, CC-32527, M-31806, MY-37765 CDs: MYK-37765, SFK-46712, MLK-69249 SMK-60175
Prokofiev, Sergey	*Romeo and Juliet, op. 64* (Mitropoulos)	11/11/1957 LPs: MS-6023, ML-5267, 32-16-0038, 32-16-0037, MP-38772 CDs: MPK-45557
Prokofiev, Sergey	*Scythian Suite, op. 20* (Bernstein)	5/2/1964 LPs: MS-7221 CDs: SMK-47607
Prokofiev, Sergey	*Symphony No. 5 in B-flat Major, op. 100* (Bernstein)	2/7,15/1966 LPs: MS-7005, ML-6405 CDs: SMK-47602
Ravel, Maurice	*Boléro* (Bernstein)	1/27/1958 LPs: MP-38751 CDs: MPK-44846, SM3K-45842
Ravel, Maurice	*Daphnis and Chloé* (Bernstein)	3/13/1961 LPs: MS-6260, ML-5660 CDs: SMK-47604

Ravel, Maurice	*Daphnis and Chloé: Suite No. 2* (Bernstein)	3/13/1961 LPs: MS-6754, ML-6154, M-31847, MY-36714; also in box MYX-39141 CDs: MYK-36714, SMK-47603, SBK-64111, SMK-60565
Ravel, Maurice	*La Valse* (Bernstein)	1/6/1958 LPs: MS-6011, ML-5293, M-31847, MY-36714; also in box MYX-39141 CDs: MYK-36714
Ravel, Maurice	*Rhapsodie Espagnole* (Bernstein)	1/27/1958 LPs: MS-6011, ML-5293
Respighi, Ottorino	*Feste Romane* (Bernstein)	3/19/1968 LPs: MS-7448, KS-7448 CDs: SMK-60174
Respighi, Ottorino	*The Fountains of Rome* (Barbirolli)	1/21/1939 78s: M-576 (15483/84), DM-576 (18450/51) CDs: Pearl GEMM CDS-9922, Dutton CDEA 5019
Respighi, Ottorino	*The Pines of Rome* (Bernstein)	2/17/1970 LPs: MS-7448, KS-7448 CDs: SMK-60174
Revueltas, Silvestre	*Sensemayá* (Bernstein)	2/6/1963 LPs: MS-6514, ML-5914 CDs: SMK-47544, SMK-60571
Rimsky-Korsakov, Nikolay	*Capriccio Espagnole, op. 34* (Bernstein)	5/2/1959 LPs: MS-6080, ML-5401, MY-36728, SGS-1, SGM-1 CDs: MYK-36728, SMK-47595, SMK-60737, MLK-69250
Rimsky-Korsakov, Nikolay	*Le Coq d'Or: Suite* (Beecham)	5/13/1942 CDs: MH2K-63366

Rimsky-Korsakov, Nikolay	*Scheherazade, op. 35* (Bernstein)	2/16/1959 LPs: MS-6069, ML-5387, M-31802, MY-38476 CDs: MYK-38476, SMK-47605, SMK-60737
Schuman, William	*New England Triptych* (Kostelanetz)	3/15/1958 LPs: MS-6040, ML-5347, CSP-91A02007 CDs: SBK-63034
Schumann, Robert	*Symphony No. 2 in C Major, op. 61* (Bernstein)	10/10/1960 LPs: MS-6448, ML-5848, D3S-725, D3L-325 CDs: SMK-47611
Scriabin, Alexander	*Symphony No. 4, op. 54"Poem of Ecstasy"* (Mitropoulos)	4/20/1953 LPs: ML-4731, P-14184e
Scriabin, Alexander	*Symphony No. 4, op. 54 "Poem of Ecstasy"* (Boulez)	10/16/1972 CDs: SM2K-64100
Shostakovich, Dmitry	*Concerto for Piano, Trumpet, and Orchestra No. 1 in C Minor, op. 35* (Bernstein)	4/8/1962 LPs: MS-6392, ML-5792, MP-38892 CDs: SMK-47618, Philips 2PM2-456 934
Shostakovich, Dmitry	*Symphony No. 5 in D Minor, op. 47* (Bernstein)	10/20/1959 LPs: MS-6115, ML-5445, MY-37218 CDs: MYK-37218, MK-44711, SMK-47615 (also in SX4K-64206), SMK-61841, SBK-64117QQ
Shostakovich, Dmitry	*Symphony No. 5 in D Minor, op. 47* (Mitropoulos)	12/1/1952 LPs: ML-4739, P-14185e
Shostakovich, Dmitry	*Symphony No. 7 in C Major, op. 60* (Bernstein)	10/22–23/1962 LPs: M2S-722, M2L-322 CDs: MK-44855, SMK-47616 (also in SX4K-64206)

Shostakovich, Dmitry *Symphony No. 9 in E-flat*   10/19/1965
    Major, op. 70   LPs: M-31307
    (Bernstein)   CDs: MK-44711,
                                   SMK-47615
                                   (also in SX4K-64206), SMK-61841

Strauss, Richard   *Also Sprach Zarathustra, op. 30*   10/5/1970
    (Bernstein)   LPs: M-30443,
                                     MQ-30443, MG-33707
                                     CDs: SMK-47626

Strauss, Richard   *Don Juan, op. 20*   2/3/1963
    (Bernstein)   LPs: MS-6822, ML-6222,
                                     MG-33707
                                     CDs: SMK-47626

Strauss, Richard   *Don Juan, op. 20*   12/29/1952
    (Walter)   LPs: ML-4650, ML-5338,
                                     WZ-2
                                     CDs: SMK-64466,
                                     SX10K-66247

Strauss, Richard   *Don Quixote, op. 35*   11/14/1943
    (Bernstein)   LPs: NYP-83 1/2
                                     CDs: 19054-1196

Strauss, Richard   *Don Quixote, op. 35*   10/24/1968
    (Bernstein)   LPs: M-30067, MG-33707
                                     CDs: SMK-47625

Strauss, Richard   *Symphonia Domestica, op. 53*   12/23/1945
    (Walter)   CDs: NYP-9706 in set NYP-9701 (10 CDs)

Strauss, Richard   *Till Eulenspiegel, op. 28*   4/20/1959
    (Bernstein)   LPs: MS-6225, ML-5625,
                                     MS-6441, ML-5841,
                                     MS-6822, ML-6222,
                                     MS-7165, D3S-785,
                                     MG-33707
                                     CDs: SMK-47626

Strauss, Richard   *Tod und Verklärung, op. 24*   12/2/1956
    (Mitropoulos)   LPs: NYP-81 1/2

Strauss, Richard   *Tod und Verklärung, op. 24*   12/29/1952
    (Walter)   LPs: ML-4650, ML-5338
                                     CDs: SMK-64466,
                                     SX10K-66247

Stravinsky, Igor	*The Firebird: Suite (1919)* (Bernstein)	1/28/1957 LPs: MS-6014, ML-5182, MG-30269, MY-37221 CDs: MYK-37221, SMK-47605, SMK-60694, SBK-64113
Stravinsky, Igor	*The Firebird: Suite (1945)* (Stravinsky)	1/28/1946 LPs: ML-4046, ML-4882 CDs: Pearl GEMM CDS 9292
Stravinsky, Igor	*Petrouchka (1911)* (Boulez)	5/11/1971 LPs: M-31076, MQ-31076, J.23AC-577 CDs: MK-42395, SMK-64109
Stravinsky, Igor	*Petrouchka (1911)* (Mitropoulos)	3/5/1951 LPs: ML-4438, P-14169e
Stravinsky, Igor	*Petrouchka (rev. 1947)* (Bernstein)	5/5/1969 LPs: MG-30269, MY-37221 CDs: MYK-37221, SMK-47629
Stravinsky, Igor	*Petrouchka:* Suite (Stravinsky)	4/4/1940 78s: 11389/90-D in set X-177, 11429/30-D in set MX-177 LPs: ML-4047 CDs: Pearl GEMM CDS 9292
Stravinsky, Igor	*Pulcinella:* Suite (Bernstein)	3/28/1960 LPs: MS-6329, ML-5729 CDs: MK-44709, SMK-47628
Stravinsky, Igor	*Le Sacre du Printemps* (Bernstein)	1/20/1958 LPs: MS-6010, ML-5277, D2S-749, D2L-349, MG-30269 CDs: MK-44709, SMK-47629

Stravinsky, Igor	*Le Sacre du Printemps* (Stravinsky)	4/4/1940 LPs: ML-4092, ML-4882 CDs: Pearl GEMM CDS 9292
Stravinsky, Igor	*The Song of the Nightingale* (Bernstein)	12/16/1956 CDs: NYP-2004 in set NYP 2003/13
Tchaikovsky, Pyotr Il'yich	*Capriccio Italien, op. 45* (Bernstein)	2/16/1960 LPs: MS-6258, ML-5658, MS-6477, ML-5877, MS-6827, ML-6227, MS-7513, MG-31264, MG-33270, MY-36728, Columbia House set 3P-6871 CDs: MYK-36728, MLK-39440, SMK-47595, SMK-61556
Tchaikovsky, Pyotr Il'yich	*Overture 1812, op. 49* (Bernstein)	10/2/1962 LPs: MS-6477, ML-5877, MS-6827, ML-6227, D3S-818, MS-7503, MG-31264, MQ-32055, MG-33270, MY-36723 also in box MYX-39141, M-39433 CDs: MYK-36723, MLK-39433, SMK-47634 (also in SX5K-64208), MLK-64055
Tchaikovsky, Pyotr Il'yich	*Symphony No. 4 in F Minor, op. 36* (Barenboim)	1/25/1971 LPs: M-30572
Tchaikovsky, Pyotr Il'yich	*Symphony No. 4 in F Minor, op. 36* (Bernstein)	9/30/1958 LPs: MS-6035, ML-5332, D3S-781 CDs: SMK-61556
Tchaikovsky, Pyotr Il'yich	*Symphony No. 5 in E Minor, op. 64* (Bernstein)	5/16/1960 LPs: MS-6312, ML-5712, D3S-781 CDs: SMK-47634 (also in SX5K-64208)

Tchaikovsky, Pyotr Il'yich	*Symphony No. 6 in B Minor, op. 74* (Bernstein)	2/11/1964 LPs: MS-6689, ML-6089, D3S-781 CDs: SMK-47635 (also in SX5K-64208)
Tchaikovsky, Pyotr Il'yich	*Symphony No. 6 in B Minor, op. 74* (Mitropoulos)	11/11/1957 LPs: MS-6006 (also in set STEREO-1), ML-5235, 32-16-0216 CDs: MPK-45699
Varèse, Edgard	*Arcana* (Bernstein)	11/29/1958 CDs: NYP-2008 in set NYP-2003/13
Verdi, Giuseppe	*Aida: Grand March* (Bernstein)	1/24/1968 LPs: MS-7271, MG-35919 CDs: MLK-44724, MDK-45734, SMK-47600, SMK-63154, SMK-64076
Vivaldi, Antonio	*Concerto for Diverse Instruments in C Major, RV. 558 (arr. Casella)* (Bernstein)	12/15/1958 LPs: MS-6131, ML-5459 CDs: SMK-47642, SMK-63161
Wagner, Richard	*Parsifal: Prelude to Act 1* (Reiner)	11/22/1938 78s: World's Greatest Music SR-12/13 CDs: Pearl GEMM CDS-9922, Dante LYS-083
Wagner, Richard	*Die Walküre: The Ride of the Valkyries* (Bernstein)	10/26/1967 78s: 50161 LPs: Columbia BM-13 CDs: Pearl GEMM CDS-9922
Webern, Anton	*Six Pieces for Orchestra, op. 6 (rev. 1928)* (Bernstein)	1/19/1958 CDs: NYP-2005 in set NYP 2003/13

APPENDIX F

Bibliography of Music Publications by William Vacchiano

Advanced Etudes for Trumpet, for Ear Training and Accuracy. Montrose, California: Balquhidder Music, 2004.

Bugle Calls. Denver: Tromba Publications, 1998.

The Art of Bel Canto (singing style) for Trumpet. Portland, Maine: Manduca Music, 1999.

The Art of Double Tonguing. New York: C. F. Peters, 1998.

The Art of Solo Playing for Trumpet. Denver: Tromba Publications, 1998.

The Art of Triple Tonguing. New York: C. F. Peters, 1998.

Comprehensive Trumpet Studies. New York: Vacch Press, 2004.

Brandt, Vassily. *Etudes for Trumpet (Orchestra Etudes and Last Etudes).* Ed. William Vacchiano. Los Angeles: Universal, 1965.

Graduate Studies for Trumpet, As Taught at The Juilliard School. Denver: Tromba Publications, nd.

Improvisations Based on Nursery Rhythms and The Marine's Hymn for Trumpet or Cornet. Portland, Maine: Manduca Music, 1998.

Miniature Variations on "The Carnival of Venice" for Piccolo or E-flat Trumpet. New York: C. F. Peters, 1999.

Miniature Variations on "The Carnival of Venice" for Solo Trumpet. New York: C. F. Peters, 1996.

Moving Transposition. New York: C. F. Peters, 2005.

Necessary Technique for B-flat Trumpet. Portland, Maine: Manduca Music, 1998.

Orchestral Rhythms for B-flat Trumpet. Montrose, California: Balquhidder Music, 1997.

Trumpet Routines. New York: Charles Colin, 1994.

Suppli-Bilities, Advanced Technical Drills for Suppleness and Agility. New York: Vacch Press, 2004.

Studies in Waltz Tempo. New York: Vacch Press, 2005.

A Study of Intervals for Trumpet. Portland, Maine: Manduca Music, 1998.

Bach, Johann Sebastian, *Concerto in A Minor (BWV 1056).* Arr. William Vacchiano. New York: Charles Colin, 1994.

————. *Concerto in C Major (BWV 1053).* Arr. William Vacchiano. New York: Charles Colin, 1994.

————. *Concerto in C Major (BWV 1054).* Arr. William Vacchiano. New York: Charles Colin, 1994.

————. *Concerto in D Minor (BWV 1052).* Arr. William Vacchiano. New York: Charles Colin, 1994.

————. *Concerto in E Minor (BWV 1058).* Arr. William Vacchiano. New York: Charles Colin, 1994.

————. *Concerto in F Major (BWV 1055).* Arr. William Vacchiano. New York: Charles Colin, 1994.

APPENDIX G

The Students of William Vacchiano[2]

A

John Abrahamson
Mark Adler
J. Ailey
W. Carl Albach
Jeffrey Albright
Joseph Albright
Joseph Alessi, Sr.
Jesse Alexander
Ralph Aliano
Dean Alspaugh
Edward Altshuler
Richard Ames
Edward Ampusat
Donald Angelica
David Anderson
Janis Anderson
Lane Anderson
Ronald Anderson
Joseph Andrucci
Joseph Andruzak
Lorenzo Angelo
Marc Angelone
George Apostolos
Irwin Applebaum
John Arant
Charles Arena
Jerome Austin

Anthony Aversa
Kenneth Ayden

B

Stephen Badalamenti
Alejandro Bacilar
Sydney Baker
David Baldwin
Neil Balm
Nelson Balsamo
Richard Barnes
Charles Barney
Andrew Baron
Jack Bass
Joseph Bass
Donald Batchelder
Marc Bedell
Robert Belosic
Donald Benedetti
Brian Benson
Michael Benvengo
George Berardinelli
Geoffrey Bergler
Martin Berinbaum
Richard Berlin
Lynn Berman
Donald Bigelow
Carol Bird

Howard Birnbaum
Neil Birnbaum
Edwin Bischoff
R. Bischoff
Ronald Blais
Halward Blegen
Luther Blodgett
Jerry Blum
Melvin Blumenthal
Michael Blutman
Alger La Bo
Leamon Boler
Michael Bollati
Francis Bonny
Robert Boudreau
John Bourque
Irvin Bourque
William Boyd
George Brachman
Charles Brady
George Brandt
Laurine Breitenbucher
Edward Bristow
Melvyn Broiles
Llewelyn Bromfield
Robert Brooks
Allen Brown
Nancy Brown

Barry Browner
Jack Bryant
Robert Bryant
Michael Buglio
Richard Burn
Stephen Burns
Hugh Burritt
Ralph Burrows
Richard Burt
Charles Bumcroft
Alfred Buswell
Donald Byrd

C

Joseph Calario
Norman Canter
Michael Caprella
Marvin Cardo
Michael Carl
Jules Carlyle
David Carmisi
Edward Carney
Edward Carroll
Margaret Carroll
Mario Casanova
Joseph Cascone
Christopher Casper
Anthony Cataneo
Joseph Catania
Trudy Cavallo
Anthony Caviglia
Frank Cervino
David Champion
Stephen Chenette
Curt Christensen
Kenneth Cifone
David Clark
Elizabeth Clark
Georgette Clarke
Brian Cohen
Justin Cohen

Norman Cohen
Paul Cohen
Sidney Cohen
John Colbert
Ward Cole
Cecil Collins
Philip Collins
James Concannon
William Connelly
Ralph Conz
Brian Coogan
Robert Copeland
Paul Costanzo
Iris Couiliard
Ruth Cove
Peter Crino
Timothy Cubbage
Robert Cummings

D

Arnold Daitch
Barry Davidson
Miles Davis
Robert Day
Merrill Debski
Dominick De Gangi
Edward De Groat
Marreill Delcatz
Winifred Del Merrico
Paul De Marco
Joseph De Mare
Gregory Denny
Russell Deverest
Vincent Di Dea
Ernest Di Falco
Paul Di Franco
Dominick Di Gange
Christopher Di Meglio
John Di Petrillo
Mark Dodson
Kenneth Dono

James Dooley
Faith Doss
Pricilla Douglas
Louis Drake
Lauren Draper
Barry Drewes
Edward Driver
Raymond Dryburg
Seth Dryer
Frederick Durer
Rolla Durham
Fredrick Dweir
James Dyson
Paul Dyson

E

George Eckenrode
Stephen Eder
Merrill Edison
David Edward
Randall Edwards
Walford Edwards
Lawrence Elam
Mercer Ellington
George Elliott
Lloyd Ellis
Donald Elton
Bruce Engel
Lawrence Etkin

F

John Falconieri
Steven Falker
Maurice Faulkner
Marvin Feman
Brian Fenovich
Angel Fernandez
John Ferraiolo
Joseph Ferrante
Alice Fila
Cherry Folger

Claude Fontanella
Kenneth Force
Daniel Forlano
Gregory Forlter
Carmine Fornarotto
George Foss
Robert Fournier
Laurine Fox
Kenneth Fradley
Marston La France
Lisa Franz
Thomas Freas
Allan Freilich
Barry Freios
Paul Freitas
Richard Frevert
Robert Friend
Scott Friend
Barney Fries
Thomas Fries
Lance Fritter
Edward Fuchs

G
Mark Gaber
Robert Gandara-
Barnett
William Gannon
John Gardner
Patrick Garrett
Dorinda Gay
Mitchell Geller
John Gemsky
Charles Genduso
John Gentowski
Frank George
Gerald Gewiss
Armando Ghitalla
Robert Gian
Richard Giangiulio
William Gilfry

Anthony Giliberti
Timothy Girdler
Michael Gisondi
Stephen Gitto
John Glasel
Robert Glasgow
George Glassen
Timothy Glidden
David Glukh
Pnina God
R. Chandler Goetting
Leonard Goines
Martin Goldbaum
Henry Golis
David Gordon
Gary Goren
Susan Gormley
John Gosling
Robert Gotthoffer
Leonard Gottschalk
Richard Gradone
Charles Graulich
Joseph Greco
Donald Green
Joel Greenberger
Morris Greenwald
Donald Grimaldi
Salvatore Grimaldi
Mario Guarneri
Enzo Gugliazzo
Morton Gutoff
Eugene Gutowski
Gary Guzio

H
Bruce Haberman
Robert Haley
John Hall
Ralph Hall
Michael Halpern
James Hamlin

Richard Harl
Kenneth Hayden
John Healy
Douglas Hedwig
Robert Heinrich
Edward Helbein
Robert Helmacy
Leonard Henkle
Alex Hersheman
Eugene Hicks
Caroline Higbee
Edward Higgins
Merrimon Hipps
Sol Hirshberg
Tadd Hoffman
Jack Holland
Edward Hood
Bruce Hopkins
Frank Hosticka
Knud Hovalt
Lester Hrbek
Edward Hume
Grant Hungerford
John Hunt
James Hustis
Ruth Hyatt
Michael Hyppe

I
John Ieule
Mark Inouye
Lauren Isley

J
Richard Jackson
Robert Jackson
David Jandorf
George Jansen
Dennis Jeeter
Mitchell Jellen
Harry Jenkins

Arthur Johnson
Kirby Jolly
Charles Jones
Jonah Jones
Robert Jones
William Jones
Betty Jordan
Richard Judson
Paul Juette
Johannes Jullens
Juliet Just

K
Murray Kahn
Joseph Kaminsky
Richard Kane
George Karmazyn
Robert Karon
Daniel Karp
Theodore Kasckow
Abraham Katz
Irwin Katz
Sidney Katz
Fredrick Kaufman
Andrew Kemp
Fred Kershko
Ralph Kessler
Rawson Kingsley
William Kirby
Sheffield Klein
Mary Knight
Gerald Kocher
Steven Koeppel
Norton Krasnoff
David Krauss
Martin Krofla
Howard Kruskol
Daniel Kuehn
David Kuehn
Gene Kuntz
John Kusinski

Donald Kutik
Richard Kutik

L
Carl Lakes
James Lambert
John Lambert
Robert Landholt
Alfred Lang
Jack Laumer
Manuel Laureano
Robert Leist
Robert Leive
William Lenz
Timothy Lester
Robert Levenson
Stephen Levine
Edward Lewis
Gene Lewis
Frank Liberti
Harold Lieberman
Albert Ligotti
Douglas Lindsay
Seymour Lipschutz
Timothy Lister
Daniel Little
William Lockett
James Lombardi
Ann Lomozik
Howard Long
Stewart Long
Angelo Lorenzo
Joseph Losh
Paul Loxtercamp
Ira Lubin
Jerry Lucadamo
Hans Lunde
Placido Lutri
Gregory Lyon

M
William Maddox
Leonard Malley
Lawrence Malin
Joseph Mangello
John Mannone
Margaret Marangello
Alan Marburger
Mario Marcone
Stephen Marconi
Emilio Mariconda
Domingo Mariconde
Nicholas Marino
Wynton Marsalis
Joseph Marshall
George Martin
William Martin
Alfred Mattaliano
David Mayo
Jerry McCathern
Scott McIntosh
Timothy McKeown
Herbert McKintry
Timothy McKuehn
John MacMurray
Malcolm McNab
Paul Meebe
George Melrapoulos
Seymour Menchen
William Meyer
Douglas Meyers
Timothy Meyers
Charles Miller
Frank Miller
Ivan Miller
Frederick Mills
John Minkoff
Edward Mirr
Robert Mitchell
Joseph Mongelli
Kenneth Monsanti

Rosario Montagna
Jose Montenegro
Robert Montesi
Robert Monticelli
Dennis Moore
Rachel Morgan
Edward Morgenstern
Virgil Moroni
Jack Morreale
James Morriale
Joseph Muccioli
Frances Mueller
Herbert Mueller
Neil Mueller
Francis Mullen
Doug Myers

N

Alexander Nadel
Eugene Nagy
Alfred Nattaliano
Paul Neebe
John Nelson
Doris Nemeth
Pasquale La Neve
Daniel Nevins
Henry Nieminski
Hank Nowach
Charles Novach
George Novak
Henry Nowak
Steven Nowak

O

Elizabeth Ober
James Ode
James Olcott
Alan Oldging
George Oldziey
George Olfrey
Peter Olstad

Paul Oman
Mario Oneglia
Marshall Onofrio
G. Ours
Laureen Oxley

P

James Paise
Walter Paleswki
Donald Paleswki
Donald Palmieri
James Palska
James Pandolfi
Maret Panzenbeck
Robert Parker
Henry Pasnik
Scott Peebles
Jack Pento
Anthony Perfetti
William Perrett
Frank Perricone
Frank Perry
Edward Petersen
Craig Petrillo
Annie Phelan
Ruth Phelps
Robert Pierson
Kevin Pike
John Pinto
Peter Piquardio
Seymour Platt
Jesse Pollack
Carl Poole
Nancy Pratt
Margaret President
Anthony Primola
Luke Procopio
William Prophet

R

John Rachella

Susan Radcliff
David Rafelson
Louis Ranger
James Ranti
Marry Rapp
Edward Rappold
John Raschella
P. Rasher
Matthew Raskin
Philip Raskin
Marilyn Reid
Howard Reich
Stanley Reich
Florence Reilly
Donald Reinberg
Charles Reskin
Bruce Revesz
Kenneth Ricci
Breit Riccler
Edna Rimmelin
Pedro Rodriguez
William Rohdin
Ronald Romm
Michael Rose
Jonathan Rosenberg
William Rosenwater
Stanley Rosenzweig
Bernard Ross
Robert Ross
Tracy Ross
Glenn Rowan
Jason Rubenstein
Alan Rubin
Christopher Rumery
Richard Rushlow

S

Raymond Sabourin
Burton Sachs
Ira Sachs
Edward Sadowsky

Arnold Sage
Carl Sakofsky
James Sakofsky
Ralph Salamone
Adel Sanchez
Richard San Filippo
David Sapp
Walter Sarad
Irving Sarin
John Sawyer
Robert Sayer
Joseph Scalessi
Joseph Scannella
Morris Schachter
Philip Schapiro
Esther Schatzo
Garry Schauer
Aaron Scheier
David Schenk
Doris Schenk
Herbert Schlansky
Isidore Schlisserman
Jerry Schloss
Charles Schlueter
K. Schneh
Lawrence Schotter
Joseph Schuffle
Lester Schulman
Joseph Schufle
Herbert Schultz
Abraham Schwartz
Gary Schwartz
Ralph Schwartz
Gerard Schwarz
Betty Scott
George Scott
Edward Seldin
Joseph Selletti
Matthew Selletti
Vincent La Selva
Mildred Sexton

Peter Shaindler
Daniel Shapiro
Philip Shapiro
J. Shepley
John Sheppard
R. Sheppard
Bernard Shaw
Zachary Shnek
Eric Shumsky
Andrew Siditsky
Jeffrey Silberschlag
Alan Silverman
Anthony Sindoni
Nichoal Skeadas
John Skinder
Aaron Sklut
Sarah Sklut
John Smith
Leona May Smith
Philip Smith
Richard Smith
Vivian Smith
Larry Sonn
Lee Soper
Doris Stark
Richard Steele
Carol Stein
Robert Stein
Scott Stein
Robert Stepbach
Scott Steuer
Thomas Stevens
William Stevens
R. Steward
Ruth Still
John Stillman
Donald Stolz
Alvin Stonefelt
Phyllis Stork
Franz Streitwieser
James Stubbs

T

Atsuyoshi Takayama
John Tarantino
Constance Tayomina
Barbara Taylor
Ellen Taylor
Martha Taylor
Ronald Tenore
John Thiel
Ronald Thompson
James Thomson
Sverre Thonning-Olsen
Scott Thornberg
Barney Thorpe
Albert Tiberio
Stephen Tobach
Robert Tobin
Vincent Tollone
Homer Tomlinson
Ray Torres
William Tower
Michael Tranchida
Wilbur Trask
James Tuozzolo

U

Andrew Ulyate
Jack Urban

V

Lyle Van Wie
Philip Varriale
Jeffrey Venho
Warren Vernick
Pierre Villez
Shirley Virtue
Kevin Vos

W

Siebert Waldman
Rachel Wallin

Thomas Walsh
Kurt Walther
John Ware
Mal Warshaw
Kevin Wauldron
Robert Weatherly
Robert Weber
S. Weinbaum
Samuel Weintraub
Theodore Weis
Bernard Weiss
Gerald Weiss
Carol Weissberger
J. Welde
Carol Welsbach
Warren Wernick
Ned Winn

Scott Wharton
William Wharton
James White
Walter White
Scott Whitener
David Wigler
Frances Wilbur
Joseph Wilder
Daren Wilkes
Alex Wilson
Kent Wilson
Charles Winfield
Rick Winslow
William Wolfson
Carolyn Wood
Frank Woodbury
John Woolley

George Wright
Lawrence Wright

Y
Donald Yeager
Tsipora Yoselevitch
Gene Young
Herbert Young
Juliet Yust

Z
Leonard Zanni
Seymour Zeldin
Edward Zilotto
Milton Zudekoff

ENDNOTES

Chapter 1

1. Andre M. Smith, "William Vacchiano, An Appreciative Recollection on his 83rd Birthday: 23 May 1995," International Trumpet Guild *Journal*.

19, no. 4 (1995), 5.2. William Vacchiano, "Personal Notes and Memoirs," collected and edited by the author during an interview on 15 March 2004 regarding family history and clinic notes.

3. William Vacchiano, "Carnegie Hall: The Last Stop." The beginnings of an autobiography that was never finished but collected and edited by the author.

4. Vacchiano, "Carnegie Hall: The Last Stop."

5. Jeff Silberschlag and John Irvine, "William Vacchiano," International Trumpet Guild *Journal* 16, no. 2 (1991), 5.

6. Vacchiano, "Carnegie Hall: The Last Stop."

7. Vacchiano, "Carnegie Hall: The Last Stop."

8. William Vacchiano, interview by author, 22 August 2003.

9. Vacchiano, "Carnegie Hall: The Last Stop."

10. Vacchiano, "Carnegie Hall: The Last Stop."

11. Vacchiano, "Carnegie Hall: The Last Stop."

12. Vacchiano, "Carnegie Hall: The Last Stop."

13. Silberschlag and Irvine, 6.

14. Vacchiano, "Carnegie Hall: The Last Stop."

15. Vacchiano, "Carnegie Hall: The Last Stop."

16. Bill Spilka, "An Interview with William Vacchiano," New York Brass Conference for Scholarships *Journal* 6 (January 1978), 5.

17. Douglas L. Laramore, "A History of the National Trumpet Symposium, 1968–1973, Including a Study of Selected Pedagogical Lectures" (DMA diss., University of Oklahoma, 1990), 79.

18. Spilka, "An Interview with William Vacchiano," 7.

19. Spilka, "An Interview with William Vacchiano," 11.

20. Vacchiano, "Carnegie Hall: The Last Stop."

21. Vacchiano interview, 2003.

22. Sam Miller, "Max Schlossberg" (master's thesis, The Juilliard School, 1993), 3–5.

23. Miller, "Max Schlossberg," 6.

24. Miller, "Max Schlossberg," 7–8.

25. Miller, "Max Schlossberg," 13.

26. Vacchiano interview, 2003.

27. Jean-Baptiste Arban, *Complete Conservatory Method for Trumpet*, ed. Edwin Franko Goldman and Walter M. Smith (New York: Carl Fischer, 1936).

28. Louis A. Saint-Jacome, *Grand Method for Trumpet or Cornet*, ed. Claude Gordon (New York: Carl Fischer, 2002).

29. Ernst Sachse, *100 Studies for Trumpet* (New York: G. Schirmer, 1967).

30. Laramore, "A History of the National Trumpet Symposium," 96.

31. Max Schlossberg, *Daily Drills and Technical Studies for Trumpet*, ed. Harry Freistadt (New York: M. Baron, 1965).

32. Laramore, "A History of the National Trumpet Symposium," 102.

33. William Vacchiano, interview by author, 15 March 2004.

34. Vacchiano, "Personal Notes and Memoirs."

35. Vacchiano, "Personal Notes and Memoirs."

36. Vacchiano interview, 2003.

37. Smith, "William Vacchiano, An Appreciative Recollection," 29.

38. Vacchiano, "Carnegie Hall: The Last Stop."

39. Vacchiano, "Carnegie Hall: The Last Stop."

40. Unfortunately, neither the Philharmonic Archives nor the Metropolitan Opera Archives has a record of the specific date.

41. No official record exists in The Juilliard School Archives of Vacchiano graduating from IMA or Juilliard. Vacchiano entered the Institute of Musical Art's Diploma Trumpet program on October 8, 1931,

and continued studies at IMA on full scholarship until he transferred to the Juilliard Graduate School during the 1934/35 academic year. In May 1935 he transferred back to IMA on scholarship, but resigned on September 25, 1935, to join the Philharmonic.

42. Vacchiano, "Carnegie Hall: The Last Stop."

43. Vacchiano, "Personal Notes and Memoirs."

44. Various sources give conflicting dates as to when Vacchiano joined the faculty at Juilliard. According to Juilliard's Personnel Office, Vacchiano joined the faculty in 1935, retired in 1998 and gained faculty emeritus status that same year.

45. Vacchiano interview, 2003.

46. Vacchiano interview, 2003; Vacchiano, "Carnegie Hall: The Last Stop"; and Smith, "William Vacchiano, An Appreciative Recollection," 14–15.

47. Mary Knight, "A Trip Down Memory Lane: An Interview with William Vacchiano," New York Brass Conference for Scholarships *Journal* 16 (Spring 1988), 6.

48. Vacchiano, "Personal Notes and Memoirs."

49. March 11, 1936.

50. Spilka, "An Interview with William Vacchiano," 15.

51. Vacchiano, "Personal Notes and Memoirs."

52. "Bombing of Queen's Hall in London—Musical Activity Goes On." *New York Times*, 1 June 1941, p. X5.

53. Vacchiano interview, 2004.

54. Vacchiano interview, 2003.

55. Manhattan School of Music Archives, 120 Claremont Ave. New York, NY 10027. Since Vacchiano never officially graduated from Juilliard, he transferred his credits to the Manhattan School of Music and fulfilled the remaining requirements for graduation.

56. Vacchiano interview, 2004.

57. Vacchiano was later surpassed by Adolph "Bud" Herseth, principal trumpet of the Chicago Symphony Orchestra, whose tenure ranged from 1948 to 2001.

58. Vacchiano interview, 2003.

59. See "Bibliography of Music Publications by William Vacchiano"

for a complete list of Vacchiano's method books.

60. Phyllis Stork, interview by author, 1 December 2003.

61. William Vacchiano, *Trumpet Routines* (New York: Charles Colin, 1994), n.p..

62. Vacchiano interview, 2003.

63. Richard Giangiulio, interview by author, 22 July 2003.

64. Philip Varriale, Eulogy of William A. Vacchiano, 24 September 2005 at Holy Family Catholic Church in Queens, NY.

65. David Krauss, interview by author, 2 October 2004.

66. Vacchiano interview, 2004.

67. Jo Ann Vacchiano, interview by author, 19 August 2006, Tempe.

68. See "Bibliography and Sources" for a complete list of articles written on and by Vacchiano.

69. Abe Katz, "Only...To...A...Trumpet...Player: Anecdotes in Tribute to Bill, Izzy, Jimmy, Nat, Lenny, and Joe," New York Brass Conference for Scholarships *Journal* 6 (January, 1978): 62.

70. Britton Theurer, "The Second International Brass Congress: A Synopsis," International Trumpet Guild *Journal* 9, no. 1 (September, 1984): 33.

71. Joseph Polisi, presentation of Honorary Doctorate to William A. Vacchiano, 23 May 2003 at The Juilliard School.

Chapter 2

1. New York Philharmonic, "A Distinguished History," available from http://nyphil.org/about/overview.cfm; Internet; accessed 21 July 2010.

2. See Appendix A, "Principal and Guest Conductors of the New York Philharmonic, 1935–1973," for a complete list of NYP conductors during Vacchiano's tenure.

3. Spilka, "An Interview with William Vacchiano," 16.

4. Spilka, "An Interview with William Vacchiano," 16.

5. Vacchiano, "The New York Philharmonic, 1935–1973," New York Brass Conference for Scholarships *Journal* 10 (Spring, 1982), 100.

6. Vacchiano, "The New York Philharmonic, 1935–1973," 100.

7. Vacchiano, "The New York Philharmonic, 1935–1973," 100.

8. Vacchiano interview, 2004.

9. Vacchiano, "The New York Philharmonic," 101.

10. Vacchiano interview, 2004.

11. Vacchiano interview, 2004.

12. Vacchiano, "The New York Philharmonic," 101.

13. Vacchiano, "The New York Philharmonic," 101.

14. Vacchiano interview, 2004.

15. Spilka, "An Interview with William Vacchiano," 16.

16. See Appendix C, "New York Philharmonic World Premières, 1935–1973," and Appendix D, "New York Philharmonic U.S. Premières, 1935–1973."

17. Vacchiano interview, 2003.

18. Vacchiano interview, 2004.

19. Vacchiano interview, 2004.

20. Spilka, "An Interview with William Vacchiano," 13.

21. Merrimon Hipps, interview by author, 4 September 2003.

22. Frank Kaderabek, interview by author, 25 November 2003.

23. New York Philharmonic, *Leonard Bernstein's Young People's Concerts: Happy Birthday, Igor Stravinsky*, produced and directed by Robert Englander, disc 4, CBS Entertainment, 1993.

24. Laureano interview, 2003.

25. Charles Schlueter, interview by author, 7 August 2003.

26. Eileen Prager Perry, interview by author, 27 May 2010.

27. Perry interview, 2010.

28. New York Philharmonic Archives, Lincoln Center, New York.

29. Prager was a member of the Philharmonic from 1929–1963, spending a total of twenty-eight years with Vacchiano.

30. John Ware in "Honoring William Vacchiano, January 22, 1978," New York Brass Conference for Scholarships *Journal* 7 (April 1979): 63.

31. *New York Times*, 3 May 1963.

32. Perry interview, 2010.

33. Perry interview, 2010.

34. See Appendix E, "Selected Discography of William Vacchiano with the New York Philharmonic, 1935–1973."

35. Ranier De Intinis, interview by author, 19 August 2003.

36. Kaderabek interview, 2003.

37. Adel Sanchez, interview by author, 2 March 2004.

38. Hipps interview, 2003.

39. Hipps interview, 2003.

40. Karon interview, 2004.

41. Laureano interview, 2003.

42. McNab interview, 2003.

43. Ligotti interview, 2003

44. Frederick Mills, interview by author, 15 August 2003.

45. Ranger interview, 2003.

46. Abraham Katz in "Honoring William Vacchiano, January 22, 1978," New York Brass Conference for Scholarships *Journal* 7 (April 1979): 66–7.

47. Chenette interview, 2004.

48. Irwin Katz, interview by author, 11 October 2005.

49. *New York Times*, 28 March 1942.

50. R. Chandler Goetting, interview by author, 16 September 2003.

51. Gerard Schwarz, interview by author, 12 November 2003.

52. Hosticka interview, 2003.

53. Schlueter interview, 2003.

54. Edward Treutel, "Tribute to Bill," New York Brass Conference for Scholarships *Journal* 6 (January, 1978): 22.

55. A. Katz, 108.

56. A. Robert Johnson, interview by author, 23 May 2006.

Chapter 3

1. See Chapter 4, "Vacchiano's Rules of Orchestral Performance," for a list of rules the author compiled from numerous interviews in which Vacchiano's orchestral style was discussed in detail. This is not a comprehensive list, but rather a brief synopsis of the principles that governed Vacchiano's teaching and performing.

2. Jeffrey Silberschlag, interview by author, 20 November 2003.

3. Chenette interview, 2004.

4. Stevens interview, 2003.

5. Stork interview, 2003.

6. Vacchiano, "Personal Notes and Memoirs."

7. See Appendix C, "New York Philharmonic World Premières, 1935–1973," and Appendix D, "New York Philharmonic U.S. Premières, 1935–1973," for a comprehensive list of every première given during Vacchiano's tenure.

8. Laramore, "A History of the National Trumpet Symposium," 91–92.

9. Frank Hosticka, interview by author, 20 August 2003.

10. Laramore, "A History of the National Trumpet Symposium," 91.

11. Erik Ryding and Rebecca Pechefsky, *Bruno Walter: A World Elsewhere* (New Haven: Yale University Press, 2001), 343.

12. Vacchiano interview, 2003.

13. Vacchiano, "Personal Notes and Memoirs."

14. Vacchiano, "Personal Notes and Memoirs."

15. Vacchiano interview, 2004.

16. Spilka, "An Interview with William Vacchiano," 19.

17. Vacchiano, "Personal Notes and Memoirs."

18. Vacchiano, "Personal Notes and Memoirs."

19. Philip Smith, interview by author, 20 August 2003.

20. Vacchiano, "Personal Notes and Memoirs." The handwritten excerpt is courtesy Eileen Prager Perry.

Chapter 4

1. Feminine Ending: The melodic termination of a phrase on a weak beat, the weak part of a beat, or the weak part of a bar. Grove Music Online, available from http://www.oxfordmusiconline.com.ezproxy1.lib.asu.edu/subscriber/article/grove/music/09460?q=feminine+ending&search=quick&pos=1&_start=1#firsthit (accessed 22 July 2010).

2. Vacchiano, from lectures at The National Trumpet Symposium, 1973.

3. Doug Lindsay, associate principal trumpet, Cincinnati Symphony.

4. Manny Laureano, principal trumpet, Minnesota Orchestra.

5. Robert Karon, Los Angeles freelance artist.

6. Manny Laureano, principal trumpet, Minnesota Orchestra.

7. Jeffrey Silberschlag, professor of music, St. Mary's College of Maryland.

Chapter 5

1. The dates of Vacchiano's employment at Columbia Teacher's College are unavailable due to incomplete records kept during that time.

2. See Appendix G, "The Students of William Vacchiano" for the most comprehensive list of Vacchiano students.

3. A complete listing of Vacchiano's method books and compositions can be found in Appendix F.

4. Malcolm McNab, interview by author, 5 September 2003.

5. William Vacchiano, "The Introductory Lesson," *The Brass Player* (Winter 1992), 4.

6. Albert Ligotti, interview by author, 23 July 2003.

7. Lee Soper, interview by author, 10 October 2003.

8. Vacchiano interview, 2003.

9. Mario Guarneri, interview by author, 9 August 2003.

10. Gerard Schwarz, interview by author, 12 November 2003.

11. Guarneri interview, 2003.

12. McNab interview, 2003.

13. Thomas Stevens, interview by author, 15 August 2003.

14. Ronald Anderson, interview by author, 6 September 2003.

15. Vacchiano interview, 2004.

16. Douglas Lindsay, interview by author, 3 September 2003.

17. Vacchiano interview, 2004.

18. Manny Laureano, interview by author, 28 July 2003.

19. Jeffrey Silberschlag, interview by author, 20 November 2003.

20. Laureano interview, 2003.

21. Vacchiano interview, 2004

22. Vacchiano interview, 2004.

23. Carmine Fornarotto, interview by author, 24 September 2003.

24. Vacchiano interview, 2003.

25. Chenette interview, 2004.

26. Laramore, "A History of the National Trumpet Symposium," 87.

27. Vacchiano, "Personal Notes and Memoirs."

28. William Vacchiano, *The Art of Double Tonguing; The Art of Triple Tonguing* (New York: C. F. Peters, 1998).

29. Vacchiano interview, 2004.

30. Burton Sachs, interview by author, 16 September 2008.

Chapter 6

1. Vacchiano interview, 2003.

2. Vacchiano interview, 2004.

3. Spilka, "An Interview with William Vacchiano," 11–12.

4. Vacchiano, "Personal Notes and Memoirs."

5. Vacchiano, "Personal Notes and Memoirs."

6. Vacchiano, "Personal Notes and Memoirs."

7. The examples that follow are diagrams of a mouthpiece provided by Phyllis Stork at Stork Custom Mouthpieces. Used by permission.

8. Laramore, "A History of the National Trumpet Symposium," 8–12.

9. Vacchiano, "Personal Notes and Memoirs."

10. Ligotti interview, 23 July 2003.

11. The terms "under-bite" and "underbelly" are words that Vacchiano used to describe the portion of the mouthpiece just below the bite where the cup begins.

12. Laramore, "A History of the National Trumpet Symposium," 81–2.

13. Vacchiano, "Personal Notes and Memoirs."

14. Robert Karon, interview by author, 25 January 2004.

15. Laramore, "A History of the National Trumpet Symposium," 82.

16. Vacchiano, "Personal Notes and Memoirs."

17. Vacchiano, "Personal Notes and Memoirs."

18. Vacchiano, "Personal Notes and Memoirs."

19. Vacchiano, "Personal Notes and Memoirs."

20. Vacchiano, "Personal Notes and Memoirs."

21. Vacchiano, "Personal Notes and Memoirs."

22. Louis Ranger, interview by author, 18 November 2003.

23. Scott Whitener, interview by author, 6 October 2007.

24. Vacchiano, "Personal Notes and Memoirs."

25. Vacchiano, "Personal Notes and Memoirs."

26. Vacchiano, "Personal Notes and Memoirs."

27. Lindsay interview, 2003.

28. Vacchiano interview, 2003.

29. Vacchiano interview, 2004.

30. Vacchiano, "Personal Notes and Memoirs."

31. Laramore, "A History of the National Trumpet Symposium," 104.

32. Vacchiano interview, 2004.

33. Vacchiano, "Personal Notes and Memoirs."

34. Donald Green and Malcolm McNab, interview by author, 20 January 2004.

35. Laramore, "A History of the National Trumpet Symposium," 109.

36. Laramore, "A History of the National Trumpet Symposium," 84.

37. Vacchiano, "Personal Notes and Memoirs."

38. Laramore, "A History of the National Trumpet Symposium," 107.

39. William Vacchiano, "The Trumpet—Its Highs and Lows," New York Brass Conference for Scholarships *Journal* 9 (March, 1981): 26.

40. Ranger interview, 2003.

41. Laramore, "A History of the National Trumpet Symposium," 106.

42. Vacchiano interview, 2004.

43. "Joseph Alessi—Virtuoso Trumpeter and Teacher," *San Francisco Chronicle* (San Francisco), 29 December 2004; Katz, "Only...To...A...Trumpet...Player," 113.

Chapter 7

1. Transcribed from an audio recording by the author.

Appendices

1. Vacchiano appeared on hundreds of recordings with the New York Philharmonic, RCA Victor Orchestra, Columbia Symphony, and a variety of other independent orchestras. Many of these are première recordings, including both standard and contemporary styles. Among them are Mahler's *Symphony No. 5* with Bruno Walter conducting (1947) and Berg's *Wozzeck* with Dimitri Mitropoulos conducting (1951). The advent of broadcasts and recorded music set a new standard for aspiring musicians. With only a handful of recordings available of any particular composition, one could not escape Vacchiano's influence. In regards to trumpet repertoire, he was only the second trumpet player in America to record Bach's *Brandenburg Concerto No. 2,* with Fritz Reiner conducting (ca. 1949); the first being Roger Voisin (ca. 1946). In addition to the première recordings, Vacchiano recorded many works with the composer as conductor, including Stravinsky, Bernstein, Hindemith, Milhaud, and Copland. As a result of playing with the New York Philharmonic and recording albums in New York City, Vacchiano recorded many compositions more than once with a different conductor each time: Stravinsky's *Petrouchka* (four times), Mahler's *Symphony No. 5* (three times), Mussorgsky's *Pictures at an Exhibition* (three times) and Scriabin's *Poem of Ecstasy* (two times). The most prominent video recordings of Vacchiano's playing are from *Leonard Bernstein's Young People's Concerts* with the New York Philharmonic. Vacchiano was featured on many of these broadcasts, including compositions like Stravinsky's *Petrouchka* and Gershwin's *American in Paris*. For those who never saw Vacchiano play live, these videos are a wonderful resource showing Vacchiano's style and prowess in the Philharmonic.

2. This list is derived from the following sources: The Juilliard School Archives, Manhattan School of Music Archives, "William Vacchiano, An Appreciative Recollection on His 83rd Birthday: 23 May 1995" by André M. Smith (ITG *Journal,* May 1995), "Tribute to Bill" by Ed Treutel, *Trumpet Routines* by William Vacchiano, *Moving Transposition* by William Vacchiano, "Personal Notes and Memoirs" collected and edited by the author, and numerous interviews with the author.

BIBLIOGRAPHY AND SOURCES

Almeida, John, and James Shugert. "The 1993 ITG Conference: The Action in Akron." International Trumpet Guild *Journal* 18, no. 1 (1993): 4–28.

"An ITG Presentation to William Vacchiano." International Trumpet Guild *Journal* 9, no. 1 (1984): 33.

Anderson, Ronald. Interview by author, 6 September 2003, Tempe, AZ. Recorded phone interview. Author's personal copy.

Arban, Jean-Baptiste. *Complete Conservatory Method for Trumpet*. Ed. Edwin Franko Goldman and Walter M. Smith. New York: Carl Fischer, 1936.

Baldwin, David. Interview by author, 16 June 2010, Beaumont, TX. Recorded phone interview. Author's personal copy.

Balm, Neil. Interview by author, 19 March 2004, New York. Audio Recording. Author's personal copy.

Burns, Stephen. Interview by author, 16 September 2003, Tempe, AZ. E-mail correspondence. Author's personal copy.

Chenette, Stephen. Interview by author, 25 October 2004, Tempe, AZ. Recorded phone interview. Author's personal copy.

Crisara, Raymond. Interview by author, 5 October 2005, Tempe, AZ. Recorded phone interview. Author's personal copy.

De Intinis, Ranier. Interview by author, 19 August 2003, Mannes College of Music, NY. Audio recording. Author's personal copy.

Erskine, John. *The Philharmonic-Symphony Society of New York: Its First Hundred Years*. New York: Macmillan Company, 1943.

Fornarotto, Carmine. Interview by author, 24 September 2003, Tempe, AZ. Recorded phone interview. Author's personal copy.

Giangiulio, Richard. Interview by author, 22 July 2003, Tempe, AZ. Recorded phone interview. Author's personal copy.

Glover, Stephen L. "Armando Ghitalla: An Interview." International Trumpet Guild *Newsletter* 9, no. 2 (1982): 7–12.

Goetting, R. Chandler. Interview by author, 16 September 2003, Tempe, AZ. Recorded phone interview. Author's personal copy.

Gould, Mark. Interview by author, 10 October 2005, Tempe, AZ. Recorded phone interview. Author's personal copy.

Green, Donald, and Malcolm McNab. Interview by author, 20 January 2004, home of Malcolm McNab, CA. Audio recording. Author's personal copy.

Grove Music Online. "Feminine Ending." Available from http://www.oxfordmusiconline.com.ezproxy1.lib.asu.edu/subscriber/article/grove/music/09460?q=feminine+ending&search=quick&pos=1&_start=1#firsthit (accessed 22 July 2010).

Guarneri, Mario. Interview by author, 9 August 2003, Tempe, AZ. Recorded phone interview. Author's personal copy.

Haley, Robert. Interview by author, 19 October 2005, Tempe, AZ. E-mail correspondence. Author's personal copy.

Herman, Edward. Interview by author, 25 July 2003, Tempe, AZ. Letter correspondence. Author's personal copy.

Hipps, Merrimon. Interview by author, 4 September 2003, Tempe, AZ. Recorded phone interview. Author's personal copy.

"Honoring William Vacchiano, January 22, 1978." New York Brass Conference for Scholarships *Journal* 7 (April 1979): 62–68.

Hosticka, Frank. Interview by author, 20 August 2003, home of Frank Hosticka, NY. Audio recording. Author's personal copy.

Johnson, A. Robert. Interview by author, 23 May 2006, Tempe, AZ. Recorded phone interview. Author's personal copy.

The Juilliard School Archives. Located in the Lila Acheson Wallace Library at The Juilliard School, 60 Lincoln Center Plaza, New York, NY 10023.

Juilliard School of Music. *The Juilliard Report: on Teaching the Litera-*

ture and Materials of Music. New York: W. W. Norton & Company, 1953.

Karon, Robert. Interview by author, 25 January 2004, Tempe, AZ. Recorded phone interview. Author's personal copy.

Kaderabek, Frank. Interview by author, 25 November 2003, Tempe, AZ. Recorded phone interview. Author's personal copy.

Katz, Irwin. Interview by author, 11 October 2005, Tempe, AZ. Recorded phone interview. Author's personal copy.

Katz, Abe. "Only...To...A...Trumpet...Player: Anecdotes in Tribute to Bill, Izzy, Jimmy, Nat, Lenny, and Joe." New York Brass Conference for Scholarships *Journal* 6 (January 1978): 108–114.

Knight, Mary. "A Trip Down Memory Lane: An Interview with William Vacchiano," New York Brass Conference for Scholarships *Journal* 16 (Spring 1988): 4–6.

Krauss, David. Interview by author, 2 October 2004, Tempe, AZ. Recorded phone interview. Author's personal copy.

Kuehn, David. Interview by author, 8 April 2004, Tempe, AZ. Letter correspondence. Author's personal copy.

Laramore, Douglas L. "A History of the National Trumpet Symposium, 1968–1973, Including a Study of Selected Pedagogical Lectures." DMA diss., University of Oklahoma, 1990.

Laureano, Manuel. Interview by author, 28 July 2003, Tempe, AZ. Recorded phone interview. Author's personal copy.

Ligotti, Albert. Interview by author, 20 July 2003; 23 July 2003, Tempe, AZ. Recorded phone interview. Author's personal copy.

Lindsay, Douglas. Interview by author, 3 September 2003, Tempe, AZ. Recorded phone interview. Author's personal copy.

Manhattan School of Music Archives. 120 Claremont Ave. New York, NY 10027.

Mase, Raymond. Interview by author, 4 November 2005, Tempe, AZ. E-mail correspondence. Author's personal copy.

McNab, Malcolm. Interview by author, 5 September 2003, Tempe, AZ. Recorded phone interview. Author's personal copy.

Miller, Sam. "Max Schlossberg." Master's thesis, The Juilliard School, 1993.

Mills, Frederick. Interview by author, 15 August 2003, Tempe, AZ. E-mail correspondence. Author's personal copy.

New York Philharmonic Archives. 10 Lincoln Center Plaza, New York, NY 10023.

New York Philharmonic. "A Distinguished History." Available from http://nyphil.org/about/overview.cfm (accessed 21 July 2010).

New York Philharmonic. *Leonard Bernstein's Young People's Concerts.* Produced and directed by Robert Englander. 9 DVD set. CBS Entertainment, 1993.

Olmstead, Andrea. *Juilliard: A History.* Music in American Life. Chicago: University of Illinois, 1999.

Perlis, Vivian. *Charles Ives Remembered: an Oral History.* New Haven: Yale University Press, 1974.

Perry, Eileen Prager. Interview by author, 27 May 2010, Beaumont, TX. Recorded phone interview. Author's personal copy.

Polisi, Joseph. Interview by author, 25 September 2003, Tempe, AZ. Recorded phone interview. Author's personal copy.

Polisi, Joseph. Presentation of Honorary Doctorate to William A. Vacchiano, 23 May 2003 at The Juilliard School. Courtesy Joseph Polisi.

Ranger, Louis. Interview by author, 18 November 2003, Tempe, AZ. Recorded phone interview. Author's personal copy.

Revesz, Bruce. Interview by author, 9 September 2005, Tempe, AZ. Recorded phone interview. Author's personal copy.

Rodziński, Halina. *Our Two Lives.* New York: Scribner's Sons, 1976.

Romm, Ronald. Interview by author, 5 August 2003, Tempe, AZ. Recorded phone interview. Author's personal copy.

Rosenzweig, Stanley. Interview by author, 23 November 2005, Tempe, AZ. Recorded phone interview. Author's personal copy.

Ryding, Erik, and Rebecca Pechefsky. *Bruno Walter: A World Elsewhere.* New Haven: Yale University Press, 2001.

Sachs, Burton. Interview by author, 25 May 2006, Tempe, AZ Recorded phone interview. Author's personal copy.

Sachse, Ernest. *100 Studies for Trumpet*. New York: G. Schirmer, 1967.

Saint-Jacome, Louis A. *Grand Method for Trumpet or Cornet*. Ed. Claude Gordon. New York: Carl Fischer, 2002.

Sanchez, Adel. Interview by author, 2 March 2004, Tempe, AZ. Recorded phone interview. Author's personal copy.

Schlueter, Charles. Interview by author, 7 August 2003, Tempe, AZ. Recorded phone interview. Author's personal copy.

Schlossberg, Max. *Daily Drills and Technical Studies for Trumpet*. Ed. Harry Freistadt. New York: M. Baron, 1965.

Schwarz, Gerard. Interview by author, 12 November 2003, Tempe, AZ. Recorded phone interview. Author's personal copy.

Shanet, Howard. *Philharmonic: A History of New York's Orchestra*. New York: Doubleday & Company, 1975.

Silberschlag, Jeffrey. Interview by author, 20 November 2003, Tempe, AZ. Recorded phone interview. Author's personal copy.

Silberschlag, Jeff. "Studying with William Vacchiano." New York Brass Conference for Scholarships *Journal* 10 (Spring 1982): 74–75.

Silberschlag, Jeff and John Irvine. "William Vacchiano." International Trumpet Guild *Journal* 16, no. 2 (1991): 4–11.

Schlueter, Charles. "My Studies with Bill." Correspondence to author, 5 August 2003. Author's personal copy.

Smith, André M. "Max Schlossberg: Founder of the American School of Trumpet Playing in the Twentieth Century." International Trumpet Guild *Journal* 21, no. 4 (1997): 22–48.

———. "William Vacchiano, An Appreciative Recollection on His 83rd Birthday: 23 May 1995." International Trumpet Guild *Journal* 19, no. 4 (1995): 5–33.

Smith, Philip. Interview by author, 20 August 2003, Avery Fisher Hall, NY. Audio recording. Author's personal copy.

Soper, Lee. Interview by author, 10 October 2003, Tempe, AZ. Recorded phone interview. Author's personal copy.

Soper, Lee. "The Many Facets of William Vacchiano." Speech given at the memorial service of William Vacchiano. Paul Recital Hall, The Juilliard School, 11 January 2006.

Spilka, Bill. "An Interview with William Vacchiano." New York Brass Conference for Scholarships *Journal* 6 (January 1978): 5–21.

———. "Peppy—His Life with Vincent Bach." New York Brass Conference for Scholarships *Journal* 9 (March 1981): 48–55.

Stevens, Thomas. Interview by author, 15 August 2003, Tempe, AZ. E-mail correspondence. Author's personal copy.

Stork, Phyllis. Interview by author, 1 December 2003, Tempe, AZ. Recorded phone interview. Author's personal copy.

Tenore, Ronald. Interview by author, 18 October 2005, Tempe, AZ. Letter correspondence. Author's personal copy.

Theurer, Britton. "The Second International Brass Congress: A Synopsis." International Trumpet Guild *Journal* 9, no. 1 (September 1984): 12–35.

Treutel, Ed. "Tribute to Bill." New York Brass Conference for Scholarships *Journal* 6 (January 1978): 22.

Tunnell, Michael. "Armando Ghitalla—Master Trumpeter, Master Teacher, Master Musician." International Trumpet Guild *Journal* 21, no. 4 (1997): 4–16.

Vacchiano, Jo Ann. Interview by author, 19 August 2006, Tempe, AZ. Letter correspondence. Author's personal copy.

Vacchiano, William. "American Trumpet in Prague: A Letter to Frank Kaderabek from William Vacchiano." *The Brass Player* (Spring 1993): 16.

———. "A Physician's View of Your Heart and Lungs for the Brass Player: An Interview with Philip Varriale." New York Brass Conference for Scholarships *Journal* 11 (Spring 1983): 34–36.

———. "Booknotes: The 'Raison d'Etre' of *Trumpet Routines*." *The Brass Player* (Spring 1993): 4.

———. "Review of *A Trumpeter's Guide to Orchestral Excerpts*, by Anne F. Hardin." *The Brass Player* (Winter 1986): 17.

———. "Carnegie Hall: The Last Stop." New York, 1992. Collected and edited by Brian A. Shook. Author's personal collection.

———. "Chops." *The Brass Player* (Fall 1990): 8.

———. Interview by author, 22 August 2003; 15 March 2004, home of William Vacchiano, NY. Audio recording. Author's personal copy.

———. "The Introductory Lesson." *The Brass Player* (Winter 1992): 4.

———. "Mayor Fiorello LaGuardia—The Musician." *The Brass Player* (Fall 1986): 6.

———. "Max Schlossberg..." New York Brass Conference for Scholarships *Journal* 17 (Spring, 1989): 44–47.

———. "Musical Musings: On the Road with the New York Philharmonic (1935–1973)." *The Brass Player* (Spring 2000): 6–8.

———. "The Music Schools." New York Brass Conference for Scholarships *Journal* 8 (May, 1980): 87.

———. "The New York Philharmonic, 1935–1973." New York Brass Conference for Scholarships *Journal* 10 (Spring, 1982):, 100–101.

———. "Personal Notes and Memoirs." Collected and edited by Brian A. Shook. Author's personal collection.

———. "Progress in Brass: 1850 to 1950." New York Brass Conference for Scholarships *Journal* 12 (1984): 28–29.

———. "Supply and Demand." *The Brass Player* (Winter 1989): 2.

———. "The Trumpet." New York Brass Conference for Scholarships *Journal* 11 (Spring, 1983): 68.

———. "The Trumpet—Its Highs and Lows." New York Brass Conference for Scholarships *Journal* 9 (March, 1981): 26.

———. *Trumpet Routines*. New York: Charles Colin, 1994.

———. "The Trumpet Student's Position Today." New York Brass Conference for Scholarships *Journal* 9 (March, 1981): 27.

———. "Vacchiano Vignettes: The Audition—Then and Now." *The Brass Player* (Winter 1994): 20.

———. "William Vacchiano Alumni." New York Brass Conference for Scholarships *Journal* 9 (March, 1981): 28.

———. "William Vacchiano Reviews: *Escapade* by Philip A. Smith." *The Brass Player* (Fall 1989): 4.

———. "Why You Should Attend the New York Brass Conference for Scholarships." New York Brass Conference for Scholarships *Journal* 8 (May, 1980): 86.

Varriale, Philip. Eulogy of William A. Vacchiano, 24 September 2005 at Holy Family Catholic Church in Queens, NY. Courtesy Philip Varriale.

Varriale, Philip. Interview by author, 26 October 2005, Albuquerque. Recorded phone interview. Author's personal copy.

Ware, John. Interview by author, 26 March 2004, Tempe, AZ. Recorded phone interview. Author's personal copy.

Ware, John. "Nat Prager: I Still Miss Him and Will Never Forget Him." New York Brass Conference for Scholarships *Journal* 6 (January, 1978): 105.

Wilder, Joseph. Interview by author, 19 August 2003, Local 802 AFM, NY. Audio recording. Author's personal copy.

Young, Gene. Interview by author, 6 July 2006, Tempe, AZ. Recorded phone interview. Author's personal copy.

INDEX

Note: Page numbers in *italics* indicate figures.

Alessi, Joseph, Sr., 99
Alessi-Vacchiano Mute, 99
Also Sprach Zarathustra (Strauss),
    41–42, 54–55, 57
An American in Paris (Gershwin), 42
Anderson, Leroy, 115, *photo insert*
Anderson, Ron, 74
Anything Goes! (Porter), 19
arpeggios, 60, 64, 68, *69*
The Art of Double Tonguing
    (Vacchiano), 78
The Art of Triple Tonguing (Vacchiano),
    78
articles on Vacchiano, 27
articulation, *59*, 59–62, *60*, *61*, 78–79
Ashkenazy, Vladimir, 40
attack
    and mouthpiece shape, 85–86,
        88–89
    and tonguing technique, 78
    and Vacchiano's teaching style, 109,
        112, 122
    and variations of music styles, 62
auditions, xiii, 17–18, 56–58, 76, 86,
    108
Avery Fisher Hall, *photo insert*
awards, 27

Bach, Johann Sebastian
    Brandenburg Concerto No. 2, xiii, 45,
        56, 57, 106, *photo insert*
    Magnificat, 36, 91
    Symphony No. 2, 88
Bach, Vincent, 83, 94

backbore of mouthpieces, *83*, 91–92,
    99
Baker, Julius, 119, *photo insert*
Baldwin, David, 108–9
"Ballerina's Dance" (Stravinsky), 60,
    60, 65
Balm, Neil, 109
Barbirolli, John, 28, *photo insert*
Bartok, Béla, 96
Beethoven, Ludwig van
    and conductor interpretations,
        29–30
    Leonore Overture Nos. 2 and 3, 53,
        55, *55*, 62
    Symphony No. 3 (Eroica), 33
    Symphony No. 4, 19
    Symphony No. 5, 30
Bell, Bill, *photo insert*
Bennett, Louis, 4–5
Benson, Brian, 25–26
Bentley College, 11
Berg, Alban, 44
Berlioz, Hector, 42–43
Bernstein, Leonard
    and Prager, 36, 40
    Tchaikovsky concerts, 116
    tenure with New York
        Philharmonic, 28–29
    Vacchiano on, 31
    and Vacchiano/Ware teamwork, 97
    and Vacchiano's experience, 52
    and Vacchiano's leadership, 43
    and Vacchiano's musicianship,
        43–44
    and Vacchiano's performing career, xv

birthday of Vacchiano, 3, 103–4, *photo insert*
bite of mouthpieces, 85–86
Blank, Isidor (Izzy), 15–16, 44, 47
Blutman, Michael, 110
Böhm, Karl, 42
Bolero (Ravel), 96–97, 98
books by Vacchiano, 24, 78, 102, 108
bore of mouthpieces, *83,* 90–91
Boston Symphony Orchestra, 8, 29, 32
Boulez, Pierre, 28
Brahms, Johannes, 62, 85–86
Brandenburg Concerto No. 2 (Bach), xiii, 45, 56, 57, 106, *photo insert*
breath control, 77. *See also* endurance
Bride of the Waves (Clarke), 114
broadcasting technology, xv
Bruckner, Anton, 49, 62
"Buckaroo's Holiday" (Copland), 42
bugle calls, 53, 55, 98
Bugler's Holiday (Anderson), 115, *photo insert*
Bukur, George, 82
Burke, James, 88
Bush, Irving, *photo insert*

cadence, 50, 65–66
Camp Devons, 7
Canadian Brass, 115, *photo insert*
Capriccio Espagnol (Rimsky-Korsakov), 79, 80, *80*
Capriccio Italien (Tchaikovsky), 95–96, *96*
Chambers, James, 40–41, 46, 116, *photo insert*
Chausson, Ernest, 41
Chautauqua Music Festival, 17
Chautauqua Symphony, 54
Chenette, Stephen, 45, 50, 77
Chicago Symphony Orchestra, 57
chord studies, 69
Circus March (Ibert), 93
Civil War-era instruments, 102, 119
clarinet, 5–6
clarino style of playing, 12

Clarke, Herbert L., 114
Colin, Charles, *photo insert*
color of sound, 42, 46, 89, 91
Columbia Orchestra, 20
Columbia Teachers College, xv, 67
community bands, 26–27
Complete Conservatory Method for Trumpet (Arban)
    and Schlossberg's teaching style, 14
    and tone production, 76
    and Vacchiano's teaching style, 67–70, *68, 69,* 72, 109–10, 116
Concerto for Orchestra (Bartok), 96
Concerto for Piano, Trumpet, and Strings (Shostakovich), 79, *79,* 99
Connotations for Orchestra (Copland), 34
Copland, Aaron
    "Buckaroo's Holiday," 42
    Connotations for Orchestra, 34
    and historical background of compositions, 52
    Quiet City, 41
    Rodeo, 42
    Rodeo (Copland), 42
    Symphony No. 2, 34
    Symphony No. 2 (Copland), 34
Coq d'Or (Rimsky-Korsakov), 95
cornet, 5–8, 95, 98, 102–3, 114, 119
Coronation March (Meyerbeer), 34
Corvino, Alfredo, *photo insert*
Crisara, Raymond, 110
crossword puzzles, 25, 101, 102
cup of mouthpieces, *83,* 87–90, *88*
curiosity of Vacchiano, 102
cushion rims, 86–87, *87*

Daellenbach, Charles, *photo insert*
Daily Drills and Technical Studies for Trumpet (Schlossberg), 14
Dale, Dilbert, 120
Damrosch, Frank, 16
Damrosch, Walter, 7, 16
dance bands, 10
Das Lied von der Erde (Mahler), 52

Davidson, Louis, 13, 18, 47
Davis, Miles, xv, 75, 108
De Intinis, Ranier, 40, 111
death of Vacchiano, 100
Debussy, Claude, 18, *19*
Der Rosenkavalier (Strauss), 17–18, *18*
Die Walküre: The Ride of the Valkyries (Wagner), 63
DiNobile, Mr. (music teacher), 5–6, 74
Don Carlos (Verdi), 57–58, *58*
Don Juan (Strauss), 71, 81–82
Don Quixote (Strauss), 31
double-tonguing, 78–80
Downes, Olin, 45–46

education of Vacchiano
    CPA training, 11, 26, 103
    early studies, 4–10
    honorary Juilliard doctorate, 27, 104, 107–8, *photo insert*
    and language skills, 25
    Manhattan School of Music degrees, 23
    mathematics skills, 26
Ein Heldenleben (Strauss), 32, *32,* 62, 97
embouchure
    and mouthpiece selection, 81, 85, 87
    and Vacchiano's playing style, 35, 44
    and Vacchiano's teaching style, 111, 112
endurance, 44, 77, 85–86
ensemble, 33
ethnic heritage of Vacchiano, 3–4, 25–26
études, 68, 70–72, 73, 75, 102
Eugene, Ormandy, 41–42
eulogy for Vacchiano, 100–105

Falcone, Mario, *photo insert*
family background of Vacchiano, 3–4
feminine endings, 60, 64, 172n1
Ferguson, Maynard, *photo insert*
fingering technique, 77–78

Fleming, Renée, *photo insert*
Fornarotto, Carmine, 38, 76, 111
four-in-one exercises, 14, *15*
Freistadt, Harry, 14
French orchestral style, 49, 63–64
full cushion rims, 86–87

game shows, 101
Gekker, Chris, *photo insert*
generosity of Vacchiano, 111
George Barrere Symphony, 17
German orchestral style, 49, 62–63
Gershwin, George, 34, 42
Ghitalla, Armando, *photo insert*
G.I. Bill, 21
Giangiulio, Richard, 25
"Gimbles and Macy's" quote, 41, 117
Glantz, Harry, 19, 34–35, 118, 121, *photo insert*
Goetting, Chandler, 46, 112
"Goldenberg and Schmuyle" (Mussorgsky), 64, *64*
Goodman, Benny, *photo insert*
Gould, Mark, *photo insert*
Grand Method for Trumpet or Cornet (Saint-Jacome), 14, 67–68, 69–70, 118
Great Depression, 10–11, 16–17, 22–23
Green, Donald, 96, 112, *photo insert*
Guarneri, Mario, 71, 72

"Hallelujah Chorus" (Handel), 54
hammer tonguing, 61
Händel, G. F., 54
Haydn, Joseph, 62, 63
Heim, Gustav, 9, 92
Herman, Ed, *photo insert*
Herseth, Adolf (Bud), 63
Hickman, David, 1
High School of the Performing Arts, 114, *photo insert*
Hindemith, Paul, 34, 52
Hipps, Mike, 36, 41–42

historical background of compositions, 52–54
home of Vacchiano, xiii
Hosticka, Frank, 46, 53
humility of Vacchiano, 119
Hummel, Johann Nepomuk, xiii
humor of Vacchiano, 107, 117, 123, *photo insert*

Ibert, Jacques François Antoine, 93
Imperial Conservatory in Moscow, 12
income of Vacchiano, 19–20
influence of Vacchiano, xv, 108–23
Institute of Musical Art (IMA), 12–13, 16, 34–35, 76, 107–8
International Trumpet Guild, 27
interviews with Vacchiano, 1–2
intonation, 77–78, 87, 88–89, 99
Italian heritage of Vacchiano, 3–4, 25–26
Italian National Symphony, 50
Italian orchestral style, 49–50, 62–64
Ives, Charles, 34

Jaenicke, Bruno, 82
Jansen, George, xiii
jaw deformities, 90
Johnson, Bob, 47
Johnson, Gil, 41–42
Jones, Isham, 10
Jones, Oscar, 11, 103
Juilliard School
    birthday celebration for Vacchiano, 103–4, *photo insert*
    honorary doctorate of Vacchiano, 27, 104, 107–8, *photo insert*
    Marsalis audition, xiii
    memorial service for Vacchiano, 105–7
    Vacchiano's appointment to, 19–20
    and Vacchiano's performance career, 17, 34, 44
    and Vacchiano's practice schedule, 47

and Vacchiano's retirement, 102
and Vacchiano's teaching, xv, 17, 19–20, 22, 67, 72–73, 117

Kaderabek, Frank, 36, 41, *photo insert*
Karon, Robert, 42, 63, 113
Karpilovsky, Murray, 13
Katz, Abe, 44–45, 47
Katz, Irwin, 45
Keith Theatre, 10
keys of trumpets, 92–94
Klein, Manny, 13
Klemperer, Otto, 33
Kloepfel, Louis, 8–9
Knapp, Frank, 6–7, 103
Kosleck, Julius, 12, 15
Kostelanetz and His Orchestra, 20
Koussevitzky, Sergey, 29
Krauss, David, 25, 113

La Mer (Debussy), 18, *19*
La Traviata (Verdi), 4
Labate, Bruno, *photo insert*
LaGuardia, Fiorello, *photo insert*
language skills of Vacchiano, 25
LaParde, Ethel Josephine. *See* Vacchiano, Ethel Josephine (wife)
Laureano, Manny
    on phrasing rules, 64–65
    on Prager, 37
    on rhythm rules, 63
    on transposition, 75, 76
    on Vacchiano's musicianship, 42
    on Vacchiano's personality, 114
    and Vacchiano's teaching career, xv
Lehak, Jennie, 12
Leonore Overture Nos. 2 and 3 (Beethoven), 53, 55, *55*, 62
Levine, James, 53
Levine, Julius, 38
Lewiston Artillery Band, 7
Liberati, Alessandro, 6
Liederkranz Hall, 21, 34

Ligotti, Albert, 43, 70, 84–85, 114
Lincoln Center for the Performing
    Arts, *photo insert*
Lindsay, Doug, 62, 74
Lintott, Edward Barnard, *photo insert*
lip flexibility, 68–69
Llewellyn, Edward, 16
Longines Symphonette, 20
Los Angeles Philharmonic Orchestra,
    73, *photo insert*
lower neighbor rule, 65

"Macy's and Gimbles" quote, 41, 117
Mager, Georges, 8–9, 81, 89–90, 92,
    photo insert
Magnificat (Bach), 36, 91
Mahler, Gustav
    Das Lied von der Erde, 52
    and orchestral excerpts, 51–52
    Symphony No. 1, 52–53
    Symphony No. 3, 92, 97
    Symphony No. 5, 55–56, *56,* 57
    Symphony No. 6, 34
    Symphony No. 7, 94
    Symphony No. 9, 52
Manhattan School of Music, xv, 20,
    23, 67
Mannes, David, 17
Mannes College of Music, xv, 17, 20,
    67
Mannes School of Music, 117
Mantia, Simone, 17
Marquard, August, 12
Marsalis, Ellis, Jr., *photo insert*
Marsalis, Wynton, xiii–xiv, xv, 108,
    photo insert
Mase, Raymond, 114–15, *photo insert*
mathematical skills of Vacchiano, 26
McNab, Malcolm, xv, 42, 68, 73
memorial service for Vacchiano,
    105–7
memorization, 32–33, 37, 55, 72–73,
    103, 107, 114–15, 118
Messiah (Handel), 54
Metropolitan Museum of Art, 17

Metropolitan Opera Orchestra, 17,
    53, 108
Meyerbeer, Giacomo, 34
Mills, Fred, 43–44, 115, *photo insert*
Mitropoulos, Dimitri, xv, 28, 32–33,
    44, 56
money notes, 61
mouthpiece mutes, 98–99
mouthpiece selection
    anatomy of mouthpieces, *83, 88*
    backbore, 91–92
    bite, 85–86, 88
    cup shape, 87–90
    and extensions, 78
    and lip thickness, 81, 83, 84, 85–87,
        87–88, 90, 111
    and Mager, 8, 9
    rim diameter, 84
    rim shape and contour, 84–87
    and scope of Vacchiano's influence,
        xv
    shank, 91
    student recollections of, 105, 107,
        108
    throat and bore, 90–91
    Vacchiano's emphasis on, 81–83
    and Vacchiano's teaching style, xvi,
        50
    venturi, 91–92
Moyse, Marcel, 50
Mozart, Wolfgang Amadeus, 49, 63,
    92–93, 98
Mussorgsky, Modest
    "Goldenberg and Schmuyle," 64, *64*
    Pictures at an Exhibition, xiii, 30,
        64–65, *65*
mutes, 55, 98–99

Nadelson, Alexander, 113
Nappi, John, 17
National Guard, 7
New York Brass Conference for
    Scholarships, 27, 121, *photo
    insert*
New York City Ballet, 74

New York Philharmonic Orchestra
  background of, 28–29
  and conductors, 29–34
  impressions of Vacchiano in, 40–48
  Petrouchka recording, 56
  and Prager, 35–40
  principal players, *photo insert*
  Red Cross Drive, *photo insert*
  and Schlossberg, 12–13
  trumpet section of, 34–35, 92–94,
    photo insert
  Vacchiano's audition for, 17–19
  Vacchiano's career with, 17–23,
    28–48, 103, 108
New York Symphony Society, 8
The New York Times, 21–22, 45
Nielsen, Carl, 44
Nikisch, Arthur, 12
North Carolina School of the Arts,
  xv, 67

100 Studies (Sachse), 14, 68, 71, 75
orchestral excerpts, 51–52, 54–56
orchestral musicianship, 49–51
Our Two Lives (Rodziński), 32
Overture to "Oberon" (Weber), 98, *98*

Page, Graeme, *photo insert*
Pappe (conductor), 29
parents of Vacchiano, 3
Parsifal (Wagner), 77, 92, 93
pastimes of Vacchiano, 24–25, 101–2
pedagogical approach of Vacchiano
  books by Vacchiano, 24
  and career overview, 17–23
  and the G.I. Bill, 21
  and honorary doctorate of
    Vacchiano, 108
  and intonation, 77–78
  master classes, *photo insert*
  and mouthpiece selection, 83
  and retirement years, 24, 102
  and rules of orchestral performance,
    51, 59–66, 118

scope of Vacchiano's influence, xv
  and sight-reading, 49, 66, 70, 71–72
  and solfège, 5, 6, 50, 73, 74
  student recollections of, 105–6,
    108–23
  teaching style, 67–74
  and tone production, 76–77
  and tonguing technique, 78–80
  and transposition, 6–7, 49–50, 67–
    68, 70–72, 74–76, 77, 120–22
  and trumpet selection, 92–94
Perry, Eileen Prager, 37, 39
Petrouchka (Stravinsky)
  and articulation, 60, *60*
  and auditions, 57
  and phrasing rules, 65
  and Vacchiano/Prager teamwork,
    36–37, 41
  Vacchiano recordings of, 56, 107
Pettinato, John "Peppy," 83, 117, *photo
    insert*
Philadelphia Orchestra, 41–42
Philharmonic Society of New York, 6
*The Philharmonic-Symphony Orchestra
    of New York* (King), *photo insert*
phrasing rules, 64–65, *65*
Piano Concerto, op. 35 (Shostakovich),
  44
Piano Concerto in F (Gershwin), 34
piano lessons, 6
pickup notes, 61
Pictures at an Exhibition (Mussorgsky),
  xiii, 30, 64–65
Polisi, Joseph, 103
Porter, Cole, 19
Portland, Maine, 4
Portland City Hall Auditorium, 4
Portland High School, 7
Portland Municipal Orchestra, 6, 103
Prager, Cathy, 37
Prager, Nathan "Nat"
  auditions, 58
  death, 38–39
  and outside jobs, 21
  at record release, *photo insert*
  and Schlossberg, 13

teamwork with Vacchiano, 36–37, 41

and trumpet section of the New York Philharmonic, 19, 34, 35–40, *photo insert*

Vacchiano's relationship with, 111

Previn, André, 44

principal trumpet position, 49–58, 103

professionalism of Vacchiano, 73–74, 104

publications of Vacchiano, 24, 78, 102, 108

Pulis, Gordon, 40

Putkammer, Franz, 12

Queens College, xv, 67

Quiet City (Copland), 41

radio broadcasting, 20–21, 24, 28, 96

Radio City Music Hall, 11

Radio City Symphony Hall, 20

Ranger, Louis, 44, 89, 98

Ravel, Maurice
  and articulation patterns, 79
  Bolero, 96–97, 98

RCA Victor Symphony Orchestra, 20, 56

recollections about Vacchiano, 108–23

register
  high, 70, 76, 88, 89, 99
  low, 35, 57–58, 68, 70, 76, 88–89, 99, 110, 122

rehearsal, 29, *photo insert*

Reiner, Fritz, 23, 30, 33–34

religious beliefs of Vacchiano, 23

retirement of Vacchiano, 23, 24–27, 102

Revesz, Bruce, 116

rhythm rules, *62,* 62–64

Richter, Hans, 12

Ride of the Valkyries (Wagner), 63

Rienzi (Wagner), 17, 77

rim of mouthpieces, *83,* 84–87

Rimsky-Korsakov, Nikolay

Capriccio Espagnol, 79, 80, *80*
  Coq d'Or, 95

Rodeo (Copland), 42

Rodziński, Artur, 23, 28, 30–33

Romm, Ronald, 116–17, *photo insert*

Roosevelt, Franklin Delano, 16

Rosenzweig, Stanley, 117

rotary trumpets, 91–92

rules of orchestral performance, 59–66, 118

Sachs, Burton, 80

Saint John's University, 11

Sanchez, Adel, 41, 117–18

Schlossberg, Max, *photo insert*
  background and teaching style, 12–17
  Daily Drills and Technical Studies for Trumpet, 14
  health problems, 67
  and orchestral style, 49
  regard for Vacchiano, 47
  and rules of orchestral performance, 59
  and trumpet section of the New York Philharmonic, 12–13, 19, 34
  Vacchiano on, 32
  Vacchiano's first lesson with, 11–12, 103
  and Vacchiano's teaching style, 67–68

Schlueter, Charles, 46, 118

Schmidt backbore, 91

Schoenberg, Arnold, 52

Schumann, Robert, 21, 63, 92, 95, *95*

Schwarz, Gerard
  on recital for Vacchiano, 72
  and scope of Vacchiano's teaching influence, xv, 108
  and Vacchiano audition, xiii
  on Vacchiano's playing style, 46, 119

Seattle Symphony, 72, 76

Second Symphony (Thompson), 47

Seldes, Marian, *photo insert*

self-improvement ethic of Vacchiano, 26–27
semi-cushion rims, 86–87
shank of mouthpieces, *83*
Shostakovich, Dmitry
  Concerto for Piano, Trumpet, and Strings, 79, *79,* 99
  Piano Concerto, op. 35, 44
  Symphony No. 8, op. 65, 34
  Symphony No. 10, op. 93, 34
sight-reading, 49, 66, 70, 71–72
Silberschlag, Jeffrey, 50, 75
Singer, Joseph, *photo insert*
sketch of Vacchiano, *photo insert*
slurs, 59–60, 62, 76, 85–86
Smith, James, 13, 35, 44, *photo insert*
Smith, Philip, xv, 57, 108, 119, *photo insert*
Smith, Walter M., 8–9, 10
solfège, 5, 6, 50, 73, 74
solos, 32, *32,* 54–55
Soper, Lee, 70, 105–7, 119, *photo insert*
Souer, Adolph, 12
Sousa Band, 8, 17
Spilka, Bill, 10
Star Spangled Banner, 29
Steinberg, William, 43
Stevens, Thomas, xv, 50–51, 73, 120, *photo insert*
Stokowski, Leopold, xv, 51, 56, 97–98
Stokowski and His Orchestra, 20
Stork, Phyllis, 24, 51
Stork Custom Mouthpieces, xv
Strauss, Richard
  Also Sprach Zarathustra, 41–42, 54–55, 57
  Der Rosenkavalier, 17–18, *18*
  Don Juan, 71, 81–82
  Don Quixote, 31
  Ein Heldenleben, 32, *32,* 62, 97
  and orchestral style, 49
  and practice scales, 66, *66*
  and rhythm rules, 62
  Suite from "Der Rosenkavalier," 34
  Symphonia Domestica, 66, *66*

and trumpet selection, 97
and trumpet solos, 32, *32,* 54–55
Stravinsky, Igor
  and articulation patterns, 79
  "Ballerina's Dance," 60, *60,* 65
  Petrouchka, 36–37, 41, 56, 57, 60, *60,* 65, 107
  and phrasing rules, 65
  and Prager's playing, 36–37
  and rhythm rules, 63
  Symphony in Three Movements, 34
  and Vacchiano's experience, 52
  and Vacchiano's teaching method, 51
Streitwieser Trumpet Museum, *photo insert*
studio of Vacchiano, 13, 100, 113, 116, 118, *photo insert*
Suite from "Der Rosenkavalier" (Strauss), 34
summer vacations, *photo insert*
Symphonia Domestica (Strauss), 66, *66*
Symphonic Metamorphosis on Themes of C. M. Weber (Hindemith), 34
Symphony Funeral and Triumphant (Berlioz), 42–43
Symphony in B-flat (Chausson), 41
Symphony in Three Movements (Stravinsky), 34
Symphony No. 1 (Mahler), 52–53
Symphony No. 2 (Bach), 88
Symphony No. 2 (Copland), 34
Symphony No. 2 (Ives), 34
Symphony No. 2 (Schumann), 21, 63, 92, 95, *95*
Symphony No. 3 (Eroica) (Beethoven), 33
Symphony No. 3 (Mahler), 92, 97
Symphony No. 4 (Beethoven), 19
Symphony No. 4 (Tchaikovsky), 76
Symphony No. 5 (Beethoven), 30
Symphony No. 5 (Mahler), 55–56, *56,* 57
Symphony No. 5 (Nielsen), 44
Symphony No. 6 (Mahler), 34
Symphony No. 7 (Mahler), 94

Symphony No. 8, op. 65 (Shostakovich), 34
Symphony No. 9 (Mahler), 52
Symphony No. 10, op. 93 (Shostakovich), 34
Szell, George, xv, 23, 28–29, 30–32, 53

Tabuteau, Marcel, 50
Takayama, Atsuyoshi, 121, *photo insert*
Tchaikovsky, Pyotr Il'yich
    Capriccio Italien, 95–96, *96*
    and conductor style, 29
    Symphony No. 4, 76
    and trumpet selection, 93
    Vacchiano performances, 116
teaching. *See* pedagogical approach of Vacchiano
tempo, 50, 54, 65–66
Tenore, Ronald, 121
Thompson, Randall, 47
throat of mouthpieces, *83*, 90–91
timbre
    and backbore of mouthpieces, 91
    and mouthpiece selection, 87, 89
    and orchestral styles, 50
    and tempo, 70
    and transposition exercises, 77
    and trumpet selection, 93–94
    and Vacchiano's musicianship, 41
Times Square, 11
"Timid Tim, The Trumpeter" (Levine), 38
tone production, 71, 76–77, 84–85
tonguing technique, 61, 69, 78–80, 109
Top Tones for the Trumpeter (Smith), 8, 37
Toscanini, Arturo
    and auditions, 18, 58
    and sight reading, 120
    tenure with New York Philharmonic, 28
    and Vacchiano's first rehearsal, 19
    and Vacchiano's outside jobs, 21

and Vacchiano's performing career, xv
    Vacchiano's regard for, 30–31
transposition
    Soper on, 105–6
    and trumpet selection, 75–76, 93–94
    and Vacchiano's teaching style, 6–7, 49–50, 67–68, 70–72, 74–76, 77, 120–22
Treutel, Edward, xiii, 47
trills, 66
triple-tonguing, 78–80
trumpet
    cornet, 5–8, 95, 98, 102–3, 114, 119
    D-flat trumpet, 95–96
    D trumpet, xvi, 36, 41, 73, 76, 91, 92–95, 97
    E-flat trumpet, 92, 95, 96, 102
    F alto (low F), 26, 93, 97–98, 99
    F trumpet, 26, 36, 98, 106, 122, *photo insert*
    G trumpet, 97
    rotary trumpets, 91–92
Trumpet Concerto (Hummel), xiii
Trumpet Routines (Vacchiano), 24
trumpet selection
    and auditions, 57
    correct selections for orchestral work, 95–99
    and Heim, 9
    and intonation, 77
    and mouthpieces, 92–94
    and Prager, 36
    and student recollections, 122
    and transposition, 75–76, 93–94
    Vacchiano's collection, *photo insert*
tuning slides, 75–76, 78, 95–98
240th Artillery Coast Guard Band, 7

University of Pennsylvania, 11
U.S. Army, 21–22
U.S. Marine Band, 8

Vacchiano, Anna (mother), 3
Vacchiano, Anna (sister), 3, 11
Vacchiano, Dominic (brother), 4
Vacchiano, Ethel Josephine (wife),
    16–17, 121, *photo insert*
Vacchiano, Frances (sister), 3
Vacchiano, Jo Ann (daughter), 16, 26,
    105
Vacchiano, Margarita (sister), 3
Vacchiano, Mary (sister), 3
Vacchiano, Megucia (uncle), 3
Vacchiano, Milo (brother), 4
Vacchiano, Nancy (sister), 3
Vacchiano, Pasquale (uncle), 3
Vacchiano, Rafaello (father), 3, 4, 101,
    photo insert
Vacchiano, Ralph (son), 16
Vallee, Rudy, 5
Van Haney, Lewis, 38
Van Praag, Maurice, 18
Vani, Vincenzo, *photo insert*
Varèse, Edgard, 43
Varriale, Eileen, 100
Varriale, Philip, 25, 100
Venturi, Giovanni Battista, 91
Verdi, Giuseppe
    Don Carlos, 57–58, *58*
    La Traviata, 4
vibrato, 42, 66, 106, 117

Wade, Eddie, 91
Wagner, Richard
    and articulation, 62
    and conductor style, 29
    Die Walküre: The Ride of the
        Valkyries, 63
    Parsifal, 77, 92, 93
    Rienzi, 17, 77
    and rules of orchestral performance,
        49
Wall Street crash of 1929, 10
Walter, Bruno
    and historical background of
        compositions, 54

influence on Vacchiano, 52–53
    meeting with principal players,
        photo insert
    and stylistic approaches, 55–56, 120
    tenure with New York
        Philharmonic, 28, 29
    Vacchiano on, 31
    and Vacchiano's experience, xv, 19,
        52
    and Vacchiano's promotion, 34–35
    Vacchiano's recordings with, 46
    and Vacchiano's teaching method,
        51
Ware, Johnny
    at Lincoln Center, *photo insert*
    and Prager, 36, 38, 40
    substitutes for, 116
    and teamwork with Vacchiano, 97
    and trumpet section of the New
        York Philharmonic, 35, 38,
        photo insert
    at Vacchiano's birthday celebration,
        photo insert
    on Vacchiano's personality, 122
Watts, Eugene, *photo insert*
Weber, Carl Maria von, 98, *98*
Weingartner, Felix, 12
West Point Band, 42, 70
Wharton School of Business, 11
Whiteman, Paul, 91
Whitener, Scott, 89, 122–23
Wilson, Alex, 123
work ethic of Vacchiano, 7–8, 22–23,
    47, 71
Work Project Act (WPA), 16–17
World War II, 21, *photo insert*
World's Fair (1933), 15
Wozzeck (Berg), 44

Young People's Concert, 36–37, 38